A LIVING HOPE

Guidelines for God's people from I Peter

FRANK M. BARKER

GREAT COMMISSION PUBLICATIONS
7401 OLD YORK ROAD, PHILADELPHIA, PENNSYLVANIA 19126

ISBN 0-934688-30-3

Printed in USA

Published by Great Commission Publications
7401 Old York Road, Philadelphia, Pennsylvania 19126

Table of Contents

1

MORE PRECIOUS THAN GOLD

1 Peter 1:1-12

This New Testament book addresses those who are facing trials. I wonder how *you're* doing in responding to trials. Perhaps you're like the two men who went moose hunting in Alaska. Each got a moose, but the pilot who was to fly them out said they would have to leave one moose since there was no way he could get the plane airborne with both moose. The hunters assured him that the previous year they had gotten airborne in a similar plane, so they tried it. When they hit the tree tops and crawled out one hunter looked at the other and said, "Where are we?" "About a half-mile beyond where we crashed last time!" Maybe that's where *you* are in handling trials. If so, this book is for you.

The Elect Strangers (1:1, 2)

The author, Peter, identifies himself as an apostle—one sent by Christ with unique authority. Later (5:1, 13) he refers to himself as an elder and a witness of the sufferings of Christ writing from "Babylon" (probably Rome).

Peter died in AD 68. The letter views Christians in the five Roman provinces of Asia Minor as facing a fierce ordeal (4:12). The first official persecution of Christianity by the Roman government began in AD 64 under Nero.

This leads many to say that the probable date is shortly before this — AD 63 or early 64.

Peter describes those to whom he writes in several ways: they are strangers in the world, scattered (Gk. *diasparo*). The term *dispersion* was used by the Jews to denote Jews outside Palestine. Peter uses it to describe the many Christians who were scattered by persecution. They are strangers or pilgrims because their homeland is heaven and they are aliens in a temporary residence.

They are also elect. This refers to God's prior choice of them to be saved. Paul says, "According as he hath chosen us in him [Christ] before the foundation of the world . . . Having predestined us unto the adoption of children by Jesus Christ to himself" (Eph. 1:4, 5). Jesus said, "All that the Father giveth me shall come to me" (John 6:37). They are a body of people out of fallen mankind who will come to the Son!

This election was according to the foreknowledge of God the Father. On what basis did God elect some and not others? Many say, "His foreknowledge — he knew beforehand who would repent and believe, and chose them on this basis." No: what God knew ahead was that *no one* would repent, unless his resistance was overcome. Fallen man, by nature, is at enmity against God (Rom. 8:7). God's choice was to take some of these and irresistibly draw them to himself. Election is a positive thing. If there had been no election, there would be no response! Foreknowledge denotes prior choice here (cf Gen. 18:19, Amos 3:2). The basis was God's sovereign choice (Rom. 9:11).

Suppose you gave a party and invited everyone on your street to come. But no one liked you, and so none would come. (That's the way it is with God and man. God invites all to come to his son, but no one likes God on his terms.) You're determined some are going to come and so you choose certain ones and urge them until they come. They come willingly because you changed their minds. These were not chosen because of anything special about them—it was not that they were less resistant—yet it wasn't by the flip of a coin either.

They come, and while having a great time they look out the window and see those who didn't come. "Look at those stupid people," they say. "Why didn't they come?"

You'd say, "You wouldn't have come either unless I had chosen you and urged it home to you until you came. You have only me to thank that you came. And the others have only themselves to blame that they didn't. I weep over their not coming" (cf Matt. 23:37).

This election was also by the sanctification of the Spirit (vs 2). This choice and purpose of God is effected through the Spirit's sanctifying work as he calls, quickens and progressively changes those individuals.

The election is for obedience to Jesus Christ and sprinkling by his blood. The goal is obedience. The reference to the sprinkling of the blood could refer to justification or sanctification. It is not enough that the Lamb (Christ) has shed his blood, it needs to be personally applied to me. This happens when I put my faith in him.

Upon a life I did not live,
Upon a death I did not die;
Another's life, Another's death,
I stake my whole eternity.

—Leland Sateren

Peter concludes his salutation with a benediction, invoking the blessing of grace and peace upon them.

Living Hope (1:3-5)

Note the call by Peter to praise and adore God in the midst of heavy tribulations. He gives his reason: God in his mercy had begotten them again unto a living hope. The first begetting was to physical life, but Peter speaks of a spiritual birth by which God imparted spiritual life. Jesus said, "Except a man be born again he cannot enter into the kingdom of God."

Hope means "confident expectation." It is a living hope versus a dead hope. The foundation of this hope is the resurrection of Christ. If he rose, he was who he claimed to be. If he rose, so shall we if we are his (1 Cor. 15:12-19).

The content of their hope was an inheritance in heaven: incorruptible, undefiled and that doesn't fade away. It is reserved in heaven, waiting for us to enjoy. In a sense the inheritance is heaven itself, since it is the Lord himself and perfected fellowship with him.

The bride eyes not her garment,
But her dear bridegroom's face;
I will not gaze at glory,
But on my King of grace;
Not at the crown He gifteth,

But on the pierced hand:
The Lamb is all the glory
Of Emmanuel's land.

— Anne R. Cousin

Note that it is through faith, a believing response to the risen Lord, that we receive this inheritance. This hope is certain because we are guarded by God's power. God will keep us believing — he is the author and finisher of our faith. He will preserve those who have truly trusted Christ throughout their earthly pilgrimage, so they may safely reach heaven and their inheritance.

Proving Faith (1:6-9)

Notice the emotions these Christians had as they faced trials (vs 6). They were greatly rejoicing in assurance of an inheritance even in the midst of present trials. You and I can have such joy even in heaviness (see Hab. 3:16-19).

When peace, like a river, attendeth my way,
When sorrows like sea-billows roll;
Whatever my lot, thou hast taught me to say,
It is well, it is well with my soul.

—Horatio G. Spafford

At the same time there is full recognition that earthly trials bring heaviness and grief. Why does God permit or prescribe these trials?

Peter mentions some reasons, one of which was to prove and refine our faith (vs 7). These trials are not to be thought strange: they are providentially ordered for good ends. The trial shows whether our faith is real, and purifies our faith as dross is brought to the surface. "I have heard of thee . . . but now mine eye seeth thee."

This process will also bring rewards at Christ's return. True believers will receive them from Christ and will render praise to him (cf 2 Cor. 4:16-18).

Peter emphasizes (vss 8, 9) that they can rejoice in trials not only because of the hope set before them but because of their present relationship to Christ. They walk by faith, not sight, but have true love for Christ (vs 8). They joy in their relationship. Note his description of this joy. Can we have that?

They have this joy because, in the end, they receive by true faith the salvation of their souls. *Receiving* means "acquiring for oneself"—salvation is in a real measure realized and enjoyed here and now.

Unto You (1:10-12)

Peter points out that the Old Testament prophets searched their own writings to try to understand God's salvation. Through the Spirit they predicted the sufferings of Christ and glories to follow (vss 10, 11).

The source of these prophecies was the Holy Spirit of Christ, not their imagination (cf 2 Pet. 1:19-21).

The prophets spoke about the grace that would come to the Gentiles. They also spoke of the sufferings of Christ—his humiliation. Think of Isaiah 53, which predicts his suffering for the iniquity of us all, his death and burial.

And they spoke of the glories that would follow — his resurrection and exaltation (cf Is. 53:10-12).

These same prophets studied their own prophecies, trying to discover the time and circumstances. They were shown that they were writing this for us, says Peter, not for themselves (vs 12).

We have experienced salvation through hearing the gospel. Think of the privileged position we are in compared to the prophets! Moreover even the angels desire to understand the things you've experienced: "which things the angels desire to look into."

Application

Have you been undergoing trials? Perhaps you have had real problems in your marriage or with your children. Maybe you've experienced economic difficulties or physical ailments. Did your faith prove to be genuine or have you tended to give up? Did your trials rob you of your joy?

When we consider these things, think of how blessed we are if we are Christians. We have a living hope! Our inheritance is wonderful and is reserved in heaven. We are being kept and guarded in our journey there. Think of how we came to be in that position — God's election and our rebirth!

Furthermore we are privileged to share in the fuller manifestation of God's grace—the life, death, resurrection and outpoured Spirit of Christ—which the prophets and angels yearned to know more about!

Surely these things should make our trials bearable. They are designed to help us know whether our faith is real and to purify it. We should be able to rejoice in our present relation to Christ and living hope in the midst of our trials.

But by way of contrast, how pitiful is the condition of the nonchristian. He has no relation to Christ, no lasting inheritance, no living hope — only a fearful prospect of condemnation.

Review Questions

1. What is the essence of the Christian's living hope?
2. What is the foundation of this hope? How can we be sure it is a valid hope?
3. What is the goal of an individual's election by God?
4. Define saving faith.
5. What benefit does Peter mention as coming to us through trials?

Discussion Questions

1. Someone has described election in this way: The devil voted against me, God voted for me, and I cast the deciding vote. How do you respond to that? How would you change that statement? How may I know if I'm elect?
2. How important to the Christian is an understanding of his living hope? What effect will an absence of such understanding have on him (cf 2 Cor. 4:16-18)?

3. A Christian businessman in serious business trouble said, "My wife says as a Christian I ought to have joy. But how can I have joy in this situation?" What would you say to him in the light of this passage?
4. If the Old Testament prophets sometimes didn't understand their own prophecies, how did they know what to write?
5. If we are not Christians, what thoughts ought to come to mind when we face trials?

2

CAN I REALLY BE HOLY?

1 Peter 1:13-21

What association does *holy* bring to your mind—a "holy roller"? holier than thou? someone who never has any fun? In this section Peter issues a call to holiness involving a real transformation in conduct. Many who are orthodox in their views of Christ demonstrate no transforming effect in their lives and seem to be unaware of the shocking inconsistency and danger.

The Call to Be Holy (1:13-16)

Peter brings out the implications of the privileged position that Christians occupy (vss 13, 14). *Wherefore* refers back to Peter's preceding statement of the glorious inheritance assured to Christians: the final salvation ready to be revealed in the last time. Because of that they should gird up the loins of their mind. Today we would say, "Put on your thinking cap!" It impresses on their minds a due sense of the importance of their duties—to learn to think like a Christian. We need a biblical world-and-life view in every area. What are the implications of my faith for my job, my home, my social life, my material resources, and so on? Holiness requires right thinking! "[B]e not conformed to this world: but be ye transformed by the renewing of your mind" (Rom. 12:2).

They should also be sober. This speaks of a life of disciplined self-control in contrast to irresponsible self-indulgence. It is a call to be moderate in our pursuit of and attachment to the things of this world, using the world but not abusing it (1 Cor. 7:31).

"Hope to the end for the grace that is to be brought unto you at the revelation of Jesus Christ." This grace refers to the perfection of blessedness that will be ushered in and experienced by Christians at the return of Christ. *Hoping* means to expect this as something you will certainly enjoy in due season; *hoping to the end* refers to the perseverance necessary in the face of obstacles. This hope is a very important part of the Christian's armor. Notice how this hope kept Paul going:

> For which cause we faint not . . . For our light affliction, which is but for a moment, worketh for us a far more exceeding and eternal weight of glory . . . For we know that if our earthly house of this tabernacle were dissolved, we have a building of God . . . eternal in the heavens (2 Cor. 4:16-5:1).

Also Christians should act as obedient children of their heavenly Father. Obedience is the sum of Christian duty and has reference to God's law. Christians are *not* under law as a way of salvation but they *are* under law as the way God would have them live (1 Cor. 9:21). Such obedience involves not fashioning yourselves according to the former lusts in your ignorance. Earlier they were dominated by their desires. One man loves pleasure, another money, another power, another fame. The ruling desire is the principle which forms the character. All these desires, as far as they are sinful, must be mortified.

Peter exhorts to holiness. Holiness is conformity of mind and will with God — thinking as God thinks, willing as God wills. This holiness is to be manifested in all manner of conversation — that is, our conduct as a whole. This is extremely important because without holiness no man shall see the Lord (Heb. 12:14).

Peter's reasons why we should be holy are strong: God's call, his character, and his command.

God's call speaks of how we came to be delivered from the kingdom of darkness. I'm reminded of the little boy who was trying to learn the Lord's Prayer and said, "Our Father in heaven, who hollered my name." That's really what happened — God called us in such a way that we came, and if he hadn't we wouldn't have responded. How indebted we are, now, to do his bidding!

God's character — that he is holy — is next urged as a motive for *our* holiness (vs 16). If he is holy, then only as we make progress in holiness can we enjoy intimate fellowship with him. We might say, "But is not our salvation sure? Are we not 'kept by the power of God?' Why all this need for obedience and holiness?" Final salvation *is* a gift, but God has an appointed method for our obtaining that gift, and it is only through persevering faith and holiness that heaven is to be expected. As Paul says, "[I]f ye live after the flesh, ye shall die: but if ye through the Spirit do mortify the deeds of the body, ye shall live" (Rom. 8:13). Note that he brings out the great source of holiness in our lives, the Spirit of holiness. The Spirit produces Christian character in us (love, joy, peace, longsuffering) but we must walk in the Spirit—rely on his power daily and yield to his conviction of sin.

When God saves us he assures us we are justified and on our way to heaven. Then he gives us a sword and shield and helmet. We say, "What do we need these for?"

"You've got to fight your way to heaven. You have strong enemies that you must overcome: the world, the flesh and the devil."

"What if they overcome us?"

"You won't go to heaven."

"But I thought you said we were going to heaven!"

"You are. I'm giving you one more thing — myself — to live within you and keep you fighting!"

So the evidence that I'm a Christian is that there's some spiritual fight about me.

Peter mentions not only God's call and character, but his command: "Because it is written." Appeal is made here to the Old Testament revelation and its disclosure of God's will. Such an appeal bears witness to Peter's regard for it as God's word.

The Call to a Pilgrim Life (1:17-21)

Peter now exhorts Christians to live as strangers here in reverent fear (vs 17).

This fear is a holy and healthy reverence for God and a fear of offending him. It is not a slavish fear but the fear of a son for his father. And again we are to remember that we are but sojourners and pilgrims here — this world is not where we expect to stay or find our portion.

> A tent or a cottage, why should I care?
> They're building a palace for me over there;
> Tho' exiled from home, yet still I may sing:
> All glory to God, I'm a child of the King.
>
> — Harriet E. Buell

Peter backs his exhortation again with reasons.

First, he mentions God's impartial judgment of each man's work. A mere profession of Christianity won't stand up — our faith must be a fruitbearing, living thing! Moreover while eternal life is a gift, the degree of happiness in a future world will be proportioned to the degree of our holiness in this world (cf 1 Cor. 3:11-15).

Second, Peter brings forward the purpose of redemption (vs 18). They had been redeemed from the empty way of life handed down to them. They had been in bondage to tradition and convention. *Redeemed* means to be set free upon payment of a price, and Peter points out that the price was not anything this world could offer, such as silver or gold. Rather, he says, it was the precious blood of Christ!

To whom was this price paid? To God, in order to satisfy his sense of justice (cf Rom. 3:24-26). In your encyclopedia you can read of King Zaleucis of the Lochrains who, determined to put a stop to a rampant crime, decreed that anyone else doing it would have both his eyes put out. To his horror, his son was the next offender. What a turmoil the king underwent! Had he been only the young man's father he could have forgiven him; but he was the king, responsible for upholding the law. Had he been only the king he could have put the young man's eyes out; but he was his father, and he loved him. He finally solved it by putting out one of his own eyes and one of his son's! The tension between those two principles is seen in the death of Christ — God's love for man, and his determination to punish sin. The difference is that God put out *both* of his own eyes — took the whole punishment due to us upon himself in the person of his son.

And his purpose was not only to save us from hell but to make us holy — to redeem us from our old immoral life (cf Titus 2:14). Shall I then counteract the great design of the death of Christ and hug the chains he died to break?

The comparison of Christ to a spotless lamb refers to his sinlessness and points to the Old Testament sacrifices which were symbols of Christ, the means by which men obtained forgiveness. Their blood was of no value in itself; but just as paper money can do for a transaction because of what lies behind it, so could these. Where men brought their lambs with true repentance and faith, they were forgiven; but the forgiveness was based not on the lamb's blood but on what lay behind (or ahead of) it — *Christ's* blood.

Peter makes the point that all of this was planned before God ever created the world, and it was for you (vs 20).

Who delivered up Jesus, Judas for money? the Jews for envy? Pilate for convenience? No, ultimately the Father for love.

Having spoken of the death of Christ, Peter refers to his resurrection and exaltation as the foundation of our faith (vs 21). God demonstrated his acceptance of Christ's claims and ransom by raising and exalting him. Thus we have solid ground for approaching God in confidence through Christ. Charles Wesley expresses this confidence in his great hymn, "And Can It Be."

> No condemnation now I dread;
> Jesus, and all in Him, is mine!
> Alive in Him, my living Head,
> And clothed in righteousness Divine,
> Bold I approach th'eternal throne,
> And claim the crown, thro' Christ my own.

Our Response to These Calls

Many who call themselves Christians certainly aren't characterized by obedience to God's law. They live according to their own desires. What about us?

Are we girding up the loins of our minds, being moderate in our use of the world, and not fashioning ourselves according to our former lusts? Has a real and lasting change taken place in our lives? Is our major concern to do God's will? Do we long to be holy — conformed to God's character? Do we grieve over our remaining unholiness? Is there any fight in our lives?

Have *you* learned to appropriate the power of the Spirit of holiness by walking in the Spirit? You may respond, "Once that was true, but I have backslidden." Then purpose to turn from any known sin by the Spirit's power and ask God to forgive and restore you through Christ's blood, which cleanses from all sin. But also start using the means of grace, which we'll discuss in the next lesson.

If in all honesty you have to answer, "No, my life is still characterized by doing my own will and I am in bondage to my desires," you need to come to Christ in repentance and faith.

> Just as I am, without one plea
> But that thy blood was shed for me,
> And that thou bidd'st me come to thee,
> O Lamb of God, I come, I come.
>
> —Charlotte Elliott

Review Questions

1. What does it mean to be holy?
2. Why should we be concerned to be holy?
3. What does it mean to fear God?
4. What part does the Holy Spirit play in producing holiness in us and what part do we play?
5. What is the purpose of Christ's death?

Discussion Questions

1. How can we learn to think more like a Christian? Have you had an occasion when you realized your perspective on an area of your life such as your marriage, or job, or money was wrong and you changed? Would you be willing to share what happened?
2. How would you advise a person who seemed to be a Christian but lacked the hope Peter has emphasized? What could be some of the causes of this condition?

3. Doesn't the necessity of persevering conflict with full assurance of hope?
4. How would you deal with a person who claimed to be a Christian but was living a life characterized by disobedience to God's laws?
5. Doesn't the idea of having to be holy to go to heaven (Heb. 12:14) contradict the doctrine that salvation is a gift?

3

I THOUGHT I WAS GROWN UP ALREADY

1 Peter 1:22-2:3

Why do so many Christians seem so undeveloped or immature? The polls tell us there are forty million people in America that claim to be born again, yet they seem to make such little impact. Centuries ago Richard Baxter lamented over the multitude of Christ's people who were like dwarfs or infants, though they numbered ten, twenty, or even sixty years of spiritual life. Perhaps this section of Peter's letter will shed light on some of the causes of this condition.

Love That Brother (1:22-2:1)

Peter exhorts his Christian readers to love their fellow Christians (vs 22). The condition of his readers is that they have purified their souls and hearts. One of the promises of the new covenant was:

> A new heart also will I give you, and a new spirit will I put within you: and I will take away the stony heart out of your flesh, and I will give you an heart of flesh. And I will put my Spirit within you, and cause you to walk in my statutes, and ye shall keep my judgments, and do them (Ezek. 36:26, 27; cf Jer. 31:31f).

The means by which this purification occurred was in obeying the truth through the Spirit. *The truth* refers to the gospel—the good news of Christ, the son of God, having died for sinners and risen, who offers such purification to all who repent and trust in him. It is *the truth* in contrast to all the false religions that abound. Their *obedience to the truth* refers to their believing response through the Spirit. He is the one who convinces us it is truth and persuades and enables us to embrace Christ.

The result of this purified heart was unfeigned love of the brethren. They have new relatives as well as a new nature and there is a natural going-out of genuine or unfeigned love toward their fellow Christians. It is a common experience of new Christians to feel immediate bonds to fellow Christians. I have been part of many types of groups — on athletic teams, in fraternities, in a fighter squadron—but none of them could compare with the love for each other and the fellowship that Christians naturally have.

At the same time, this natural inclination needs stirring up: we need to "cultivate the lovely plant."

Peter's exhortation based on this condition follows: See that ye love one another with a pure heart fervently. The force of his appeal is that, due to your purified heart, you now have the moral capacity to love—so put that capacity to work!

Their old heart was a habitation of dragons. As Jesus said, "[O]ut of the heart proceed evil thoughts, murders, adulteries" (Matt. 15:19). But now they are to love—have genuine goodwill that manifests itself in acts of kindness, burden-bearing, sharing of material resources, etc., toward their fellow Christians. Of course they are to love all men, but they are especially to love their Christian brothers because they *are* brothers. This is to be done with a pure heart fervently. It is a love constant and free from all selfish motives. The Greek word translated "fervently" is also translated "earnestly" and "without ceasing."

This love for our fellow Christians is very important and a great deal of emphasis is placed on it in Scripture. Jesus said, "By this shall all men know that ye are my disciples, if ye have love one to another" (John 13:35). This is the mark of a Christian; and since the world is to know by this that we're Christians, it is an observable thing. As Francis Schaeffer said, "This love must certainly cross all the lines which divide men, neither Greek nor barbarian, neither Jew nor Gentile, neither male nor female."

How can this be made visible? It starts with simple things, such as: when I have failed to love my Christian brother I go to him and say, "I'm sorry, please forgive me." This is the way of renewed fellowship, whether it is between a husband and wife, a parent and child, or within a congregation. It's hard to say "I'm sorry," it's even harder to forgive; but this is crucial if we are to have Christ's presence and power manifest in our lives and groups.

Do we love the brethren with a pure heart fervently? If so we have evidence we are true Christians, since this is one of the tests of life. Hereby we know that we have passed from death unto life, because we love the brethren (1 John 3:14).

Peter proceeds with an elaboration on the condition of his readers (vs 23). Their condition is described as being born again. The Spirit has quickened them spiritually. There is, as we have said, a new moral nature produced — a permanent change in the inner man. The word of God which is the instrument the Spirit uses is compared to a seed, but a seed which has life that lives and abides forever.

Peter then compares this enduring word with men (vss 24, 25). In his quote of Isaiah 40:6-8 the transitory nature of the natural creation and man is contrasted with the permanence of God's word. It is a well-known but important point that, if we want to pour our energies into something that will last, only two things will: the word of God and the souls of men! Most of the things people are living for are going to burn up.

As part of his exhortation to demonstrate observable love, Peter calls for abstention from sins against such love (vs 1). Love cannot be practiced unless we repent of all attitudes and actions toward our fellow Christians that contradict and counteract love. He specifies malice or active ill will toward others, then guile or deceit, hypocrisy or pretending to be what we are not, envy wherein we are jealous of another, and finally evilspeaking—running down another.

The very fact that he urges Christians to renounce such behavior indicates that our old sinful nature, though mortified, is far from dead. Though we have put on the new man, we need to put off the old ways. Peter's command is to lay aside such sinful practices. This involves constant vigilance and energetic effort, walking in the Spirit so we won't fulfill the lusts of the flesh. Relying on the Spirit, let us put off malice. How? By confessing it as sin, repenting of it, relying on the Spirit to enable us not to yield to it, asking him to replace it with love, and meanwhile putting on love by blessing those who curse us, doing good to those who despitefully use us.

A divorcée came to me very distraught. Her ex-husband had remarried and her children were very attracted to the new wife. She deeply resented her and, fearing the children would want to go live with her, would lash out at the children whenever they mentioned her in a positive light. I urged her to confess this as sin and do a loving deed toward her even though she didn't feel love. We can't control our feelings; but we can, through the Spirit, control our actions. I suggested something as elementary as baking her a cake and taking it to her. She wept and said she could not possibly do it. But she did, and the Spirit of God in a short time replaced the malice with love. This is the basic way to lay aside these sins (cf Col. 3:8-14).

Grow That Soul (2:2, 3)

When we grow fruit, we need not only to get the weeds out of the garden but also to give nourishment to the plants. The Christian's spiritual life must have similar nourishment, so Peter exhorts his readers to desire the word (vs 2). In comparing Christians with babes, Peter conveys the idea of weakness and the need of nourishment to grow strong. He compares the word with milk as the proper food for them — it is the true soul food! Jesus said, "Man shall not live by bread alone, but by every word that proceedeth out of the mouth of God" (Matt. 4:4). Thus Peter says to "desire" (Phillips "you should be crying out for") the word. Go after it with the same eagerness with which babies clamor for their milk! Of course the word must be *acted on* to receive nourishment — we must be doers of it and not hearers only.

Certainly this speaks to the importance of building the habit of a daily quiet time when I meditate in the law of the Lord. Meditation involves reflecting on the word of God as it applies to my life. It means rolling around in my mind the promises and warnings, the things I am told about God and his ways. I must always be asking him to cause these to be assimilated into my life, desiring transformation and conformity to his will. It means approaching the Scriptures with the attitude, "Speak, LORD; for thy servant heareth," and "Open thou mine eyes, that I may behold wondrous things out of thy law."

Suppose you ate only once a week. You'd be very weak. But today many Christians' intake of the word comes only on Sunday. The healthy child has a hunger for food, but if we don't feed him he loses his appetite. Christians can lose their appetite for the word through spiritual ill health due to neglect or sin. What is to be done? One must force himself to eat until the appetite returns.

To assist in developing the habit of a daily quiet time, it is helpful to be in a group where we are accountable to others—where I have to report on my time, share memory verses, for example. I'm in such a group that meets in a restaurant at 6:00 a.m. one morning a week, and it is thrilling to me to see men and women in similar small groups all over the restaurant.

The great reason for desiring the word, of course, is so we can grow spiritually. In what ways do we need to grow spiritually? Paul's prayers for his converts provide good goals for spiritual growth:

> And this I pray, that your love may abound yet more and more in knowledge and in all judgment; That ye may approve things that are excellent; that ye may be sincere and without offence till the day of Christ; Being filled with the fruits of righteousness (Phil. 1:9-11).

To grow spiritually is to become more and more holy or Christlike. Such growth is gradual but normal, unless inhibited by poor nourishment or disease.

Peter says that their past experience of the Lord's graciousness should make them want to do this (vs 3). It was in the word that we first tasted the Lord's graciousness, and this certainly ought to be a powerful motive to return to it!

Search That Heart

This passage calls for some heart-searching. Do we have this observable love toward our brethren? What about our brothers who differ from us doctrinally — or racially or politically — and yet are fellow Christians? Do we love Christian fellowship where people love to talk about Christ and to pray together? Ask yourself, Am I a spiritual babe? How do I measure up to the description of spiritual growth that Paul gave?

If you feel you are a babe when you should be mature, to what is the lack of growth due? Is it lack of nourishment? What is your practice of spending time in God's word? What do you feel God would have you do about this? How and when will you start?

Is the lack of growth due to failure to mortify sin in your life? Do you have malice toward anyone? Are you engaging in deceit? envious? speaking evil of anyone? Are you walking in the Spirit? Is there anyone you need to bake a cake for or withdraw a knife blade from? David prayed:

> Search me, O God, and know my heart: try me, and know my thoughts: And see if there be any wicked way in me, and lead me in the way everlasting (Ps. 139:23, 24).

Why not take a few minutes and pray, asking God to reveal to you anyone you're not manifesting brotherly love toward and steps you need to take?

Review Questions

1. Why is there not more observable love between Christians?
2. What does it mean to be born again?
3. How do we lay aside particular sins?
4. What should a Christian do who has little hunger for the word?
5. What does it mean to meditate in the law of the Lord?

Discussion Questions

1. What was your experience of Christian fellowship or feelings for other Christians as a new Christian?
2. Would you be willing to share your experience of being born again and the difference this made in your capacity to love?

3. Have you had an experience of successfully laying aside a sin against love that you could share without necessarily identifying the other party?
4. What struggles have you had in establishing a regular quiet time? What approach have you found helpful? Are there any study tools that have helped especially?
5. Take a moment and look over Paul's description of spiritual growth in Philippians 1:9-11. In which area do you feel the most need of progress? What could you do to make progress?

4

HOW CAN A STONE BE ALIVE?

1 Peter 2:4-10

One of my favorite poems is:

> Child of the Eternal Father,
> Bride of the Incarnate Son,
> Dwelling-place of God the Spirit,
> Thus with Christ made ever one;
>
> Granted all my heart's desire,
> All things made my own;
> Feared by all the powers of evil,
> Fearing God alone;
>
> Walking with the Lord in glory,
> Through the courts divine,
> Queen within the royal palace,
> Christ forever mine;
>
> Say, poor worldling, can it be
> That my heart should envy thee?
>
> —Gerhardt Ter Steegen

That poet would have us appreciate the inestimable privileges that belong to the people of God. So would Peter in this section of his letter. He has referred to his readers as having tasted that the Lord is gracious (2:3). The present passage can be regarded as an expansion on that, and we can see from our poem the importance of our understanding these privileges. They greatly contribute to the consolation, gratitude and joy of believers and thus to the drawing of outsiders.

Part of a Living Temple (2:4-8)

Judaism had a glorious temple, with priests and sacrifices. Does Christianity have any counterpart? Yes — and on a far greater scale, for it has a spiritual, living temple in which Christians not only worship but are actually a *part* of the temple.

Peter speaks of our incorporation into this temple at conversion (vss 4, 5). Incorporation comes in connection with our coming to Christ. The Greek is related to our word *proselyte*. We come to Christ through repentance and faith. Repentance involves a surrender of our wills to a new Master. John Bunyan in his *Holy War* pictures Prince Emmanuel leading an attack on the city of Mansoul, which is controlled by Diabolus and Mayor Will-be-Will. The occupants keep proposing compromises but Emmanuel demands unconditional surrender. The refusal to have Christ as Lord is expressed by the people in Jesus' Parable of the Pounds when they said, "We will not have this man to reign over us" (Luke 19:14).

Faith in Jesus Christ is defined in the Westminster Shorter Catechism as "a saving grace, whereby we receive and rest upon him alone for salvation, as he is offered to us in the gospel" (Q. 86). As my seminary professor, Dr. William Childs Robinson, used to say, "It is not Christ and our efforts that save. It is Christ alone. It is not even Christ and faith, it is Christ alone who saves, and faith is only trusting in him alone to save us."

In Peter's illustration Christ himself is a living stone, having life in himself and being the author of life to all who depend on him. Peter gets his illustration from Old Testament prophecies which indicated that the builders of this temple—that is, the religious leaders of Israel—would reject the Chief Cornerstone (cf Ps. 118:22). Peter says Jesus was indeed disallowed of men, referring particularly to the rejection of his claim to be the Messiah. Jesus predicted this rejection also:

> And he began to teach them, that the Son of man must suffer many things, and be rejected of the elders, and of the chief priests, and scribes, and be killed, and after three days rise again (Mark 8:31).

It is interesting to inquire what those builders were like. The two men who dominated the Sanhedrin, the Jewish governing body, were Caiaphas the high priest and Annas his father-in-law. Due to their influence the Jewish leaders rejected Jesus' claims. These two men are faithfully followed in this rejection by all Orthodox Jewish people today. The Baptist evangelist Billy Hanks reports that a friend of his asked one of the leading rabbis in Texas his opinion of Annas and Caiaphas. The response was that they were the worst examples of priesthood that Judaism has ever produced, but for some reason he failed to comprehend the significance of his statement. Of course, men in all ages have continued to reject Jesus because they don't want to surrender the city of Mansoul.

But notice the contrast in God's attitude and actions — with him Jesus is chosen and precious. God reversed the builders' verdict and raised him and set him at his own right hand. As Peter stated to the Sanhedrin:

> Be it known unto you all, and to all the people of Israel, that by the name of Jesus Christ of Nazareth, whom ye crucified, whom God raised from the dead, even by him doth this man stand here before you whole. This is the stone which was set at naught of you builders, which is become the head of the corner. Neither is there salvation in any other (Acts 4:10-12).

When Christ quickens men, making them living stones, he builds them up a spiritual house — that is, he is the foundation and they are built on him as a living, growing temple in which God dwells. Christ was chosen of God as the only one capable of supporting the weight of this vast edifice. As someone has said, if all the angels in heaven were ordered to fill his place but for a moment, the whole building would fall to ruins.

A temple needs a priesthood, and Peter mentions the function of his readers: to be a holy priesthood offering spiritual sacrifices to God through Christ. In Judaism only the tribe of Levi could be priests, but in this spiritual temple *all* who are incorporated have that privilege. Instead of animal sacrifices they offer spiritual ones of daily service, obedience and praise.

> Through him then let us offer up a sacrifice of praise to God continually, that is, the fruit of our lips giving thanks. But to do good and to communicate (share your material possessions) forget not for with such sacrifices God is well pleased (Heb. 13:15, 16).

> I beseech you by the mercies of God that you present your bodies a living sacrifice (Rom. 12:1).

Such sacrifices, though far from perfect, are acceptable through the mediation of Christ.

Peter carries his illustration further (vs 6) with another Old Testament quotation, from Isaiah 28:16. Note again the excellency of Jesus — the Chief Cornerstone laid by God's hands. As Paul says, there can be no other foundation (1 Cor. 3:11). Jesus himself said, "I am the way, the truth, and the life: no man cometh unto the Father, but by me" (John 14:6). This is one of the hard places of the Christian faith, but it is important that we understand that if we call Jesus our Lord and Master we have no option to say otherwise.

Suppose I were speaking to a Jew (or Muhammadan, Buddhist, etc.) and I said, "Sir, Jesus said he was the way, the truth and the life and no man could come to the Father but by him. However, I, Frank Barker, am sure that as long as you are sincere in your beliefs you'll be alright." What would I be doing? I'd be flatly contradicting Jesus. What pride! And I'd be offering my unsaved friends the fruit of my wishful thinking on which to build their eternal salvation. What unfaithfulness!

I'd like to be able to say that, because then others would regard me as tolerant; but I'd be intolerant of Christ. Real love and faithfulness require me to say, "Sir, Jesus said he was the only way. I believe he was who he claimed to be. He's changed my life. I know that's difficult for you to accept, but won't you consider the evidence for his claims? I'd love to help you do this."

Peter gives an exposition of that quotation (vs 7). Those who truly believe in Jesus count him the most precious and most valuable thing in the world, and would gladly suffer the loss of all things if they could but have him.

Peter has already quoted the consequence for them: they shall not be confounded.

However, those who don't respond in repentance and faith, says Peter (quoting portions of Psalm 118:22 and Isaiah 8:14), will experience severe consequences. God has set his king in place, and it is easier to pull the sun from the firmament than to remove the Savior from his throne.

Men stumble at Christ's claims and are offended by demands of unconditional surrender and holy living. To them he is like a huge stone that they stumble over and break themselves upon (vs 8).

Peter adds, "whereunto also they were appointed." This is a controversial phrase. Some within the Reformed camp would say that the appointment refers to the word *stumble,* not to the word *disobedient,* so that stumbling is the consequence and the punishment of unbelief and disobedience. Those who won't respond to the light of the gospel are hardened by it. Others don't agree, however, and say that the people in question were appointed to be disobedient, to reject the cornerstone.

Called by Israel's Titles (2:9, 10)

In continuing to speak of the incredible privileges Christians have, Peter employs terms that were originally given to Israel, signifying that the church of Christ is the *true* Israel of God (vs 9). Look at the description: "a chosen generation" (RV "an elect race") from Isaiah 43:20. As we have seen, they were chosen before the foundation of the world (Eph. 1:4).

A holy nation comes from Exodus 19:6 and refers to the church being separated unto God, while *a peculiar people* is better expressed "a people for God's own possession" in the Revised Version.

What exalted terms! What privileges! Christian, do you know who you are?

> Say, poor worldling, can it be
> That my heart should envy thee?

Having given us this description, Peter now discusses the function of the church: to show forth God's praises. *Praises* (Gk. *aretas*) could be rendered "virtues," a general name for God's attributes—his power, wisdom, holiness, goodness, for example—especially as displayed in calling them and in the blessings bestowed. Or it could be rendered "manifestation of divine power." The Amplified Bible combines the two meanings: "set forth the wonderful deeds and display the virtues and perfections of Him." How do we show these forth? As his virtues are reflected in us, God's character is portrayed to some degree. As we show unselfish love as the fruit of the Spirit, God's love is seen; when we are holy, his holiness is sensed.

The motivation for showing forth his virtues is the great transition which has taken place (vs 10; cf Hos. 1:10, 2:23). To appreciate our privileges we must remember what we were before. Now we are living stones, we were dead ones; now we are in light, we were in darkness; now we are the people of God, before we were not; now we have obtained mercy, before we had not.

What a Privilege

If we are truly Christians we have tasted that the Lord is gracious. Is it possible to estimate too highly these privileges? How strong a motive they are to gratitude, joy, consolation and obedience!

> Praise, my soul, the King of heaven,
> To his feet thy tribute bring;
> Ransomed, healed, restored, forgiven,
> Who, like me, his praise should sing?
>
> —Henry F. Lyte

How great a difference there is between the believer and the unbeliever! The one incorporated into the living temple, founded on Christ the Cornerstone; the other stumbling over him and soon to be broken. To which group do you belong? Simply ask yourself: Is Christ precious to me? Does he reign in me?

If he's precious, then remember that we are to present ourselves as living sacrifices to him and show forth his virtues. Moreover we must tell the millions of our contemporaries who don't know of this foundation, which alone will stand.

If Christ is not precious to you — if you stumble over him—remember that you bring this upon yourself. Calvin Coolidge was a judge before becoming president. Two lawyers were arguing a case before him when one told the other to go to hell. The lawyer said, "Judge! Did you hear that? He told me to go to hell!" Coolidge in his quiet way replied, "Yes, and I've studied the matter; and you don't have to go if you don't want to!"

Review Questions

1. What is the Christian counterpart to Old Testament Judaism's temple, priesthood and sacrifices?
2. What is there about Christ that men stumble over?
3. What is the relation between Israel and the New Testament church?
4. How do we show forth God's praises?
5. How does Bunyan's *Holy War* illustrate true repentance?

Discussion Questions

1. Have you experienced a time when the privilege of being one of the people of God came home in a special way to you? Would you be willing to share it?
2. The poem said, "Say, poor worldling, can it be That my heart should envy thee?" But sometimes we do envy the worldling. When are you most tempted to do that? What have you found to be helpful in combating that temptation?
3. Before coming to Christ were you stumbling over him? What caused you to stumble and what did God use to help you overcome the offense?
4. Peter says that there is salvation in no other than Christ. This is a hard saying to many. How did you respond to that statement before coming to Christ? How has your

attitude changed? How do you handle objections to this claim?

5. In the light of this study, what would you say to a person who was struggling with his willingness to surrender the city of Mansoul?

5

FREE TO DO WHAT?

1 Peter 2:11-17

What is your definition of freedom? Freedom is conceived of in a variety of ways in our society:

To be free from rules and moral restraints;

To be free from authority;

To do my own thing.

The Jews of Jesus' day loudly proclaimed that they were free when actually they were slaves of sin and Satan (John 8:32-34, 44). In this section Peter, while affirming that Christians are free, shows that our freedom is far different from what many have in mind.

Follow a Moral Life-style (2:11, 12)

Peter exhorts Christians to live morally. This first involves abstention from sinful desires and practices (vs 11). *Fleshly lusts* refers to the strong desires of fallen human nature—our selfish, indulgent and potentially vicious natural appetites. Paul lists some of these in Galatians 5:19-21: adultery, fornication, hatred, strife, envyings, revelings. *To abstain* means to repress them in their first rising, and also to guard against temptation. We should not place ourselves in circumstances in which such desires are likely to be inflamed. We pray, "Lord, lead me not into temptation," and then we jump in headfirst! A friend of mine has a sign on his wall: "Don't Feed the Tiger!"

Peter tells why Christians should abstain. One reason is their position in the world. As he has mentioned earlier, we are strangers and pilgrims, residing here temporarily. Our great objective here is to promote the interests of God's kingdom. We are surrounded by communities that practice life-styles that are often the opposite of the way God calls us to live. Moreover these desires war against the soul. They wage a campaign against our spiritual development (cf Rom. 7:23). We must refuse to give them a platform from which to launch their attack!

How can we actually overcome these desires? Part of the solution is to crowd them out — to fill our mind with good thoughts. Study Christian literature, read Christian biographies, listen to Christian tapes, join a small group Bible study. Part of it is to meet the temptation with the proper biblical command, as Jesus did in the wilderness. To each temptation he responded, "It is written." We must learn to do this similarly, meanwhile relying on the power of the Holy Spirit. The writer of Hebrews points out that Christian maturity comes to those who by reason of use have their senses exercised to discern both good and evil (5:14).

The second part of moral living that Peter urges is active pursuit of good (vs 12). Our "conversation" or life-style is to be honest (Gk. *kalos*) — characterized by goodness that can be observed by others, especially nonchristians. Peter's reason is that though they may accuse you of doing wrong, in this way they will see your good works and glorify God in "the day of visitation." Early Christians often had to meet secretly and their enemies charged them with immoral activities. *The day of visitation* refers to a special drawing-near of God to deal with man either in judgment or in mercy. At that time, says Peter, your consistent life-style, seen by them, will be one of the means God uses to lead them to turn to him. Conversely, think of what obstacles we put in the way of others when we profess to be Christians but display carnal tendencies, strife, divisions, materialism, selfishness, and the like!

Submit to Proper Authority (2:13-16)

Peter now exhorts Christians to submit to proper authority (vss 13, 14). *Every ordinance of man* (or *human institution*) may refer to the ordinary social institutions of society, such as state and family. The first example of such an institution is the civil authority, the king and his governors. Paul points out that the powers that be are ordained of God and that to obey governments is one part of obeying God (Rom. 13:1-7). We are to submit for the Lord's sake, for this furthers his cause by commending the Christian faith as promoting law-abiding citizens.

The function of government is to maintain law and order and to promote justice, for the punishment of evildoers and for the praise of them that do well. This is God's design also, and when such punishment is inflicted the authority is acting as God's minister to execute his wrath (Rom. 13:4). Of course if the civil authority requires us to disobey God we must obey God rather than men (Acts 5:29). And if the civil authority has become so corrupt that it is subverting the ends for which God ordained government, and if there seems to be no possibility of rectifying the situation except by revolution: if there is real prospect of a change for the better in this fashion, a Christian could join such an effort. Think of the situation behind the iron curtain, for instance. But we should be very careful: when Peter wrote this, the man on the throne was Nero!

Peter's reasoning is that such obedience is God's will because it will tend to silence your enemies (vs 15). If you have been accused of being bad subjects, such compliance will demonstrate otherwise.

In this connection Peter issues a caution: Christian liberty is not license (vs 16). He was concerned about the abuse of Christian freedom. Christians are free — they were once slaves of sin and Satan; but they are not to use that freedom as a cover for evil. A cloak of maliciousness is something by which we attempt to hide from others or ourselves the true character of our evil actions. Saul disobeyed God and cloaked it with the pretext that he was saving the livestock to sacrifice to the Lord (1 Sam. 15:15). Though free we are always servants of God, and he would have us demonstrate this by freely choosing to be law-abiding. Freedom is not just being able to do what we want to do: true freedom is wanting to do, and being able to do, what we ought to do. David said, "I will walk at liberty: for I seek thy precepts" (Ps. 119:45). Even the Christian sometimes thinks of himself as restricted by God's laws, looks longingly at the world's false view of freedom and tugs at the reins.

Give to Each His Due (2:17)

Peter now gives a summation of the Christian's duty in various relations. We are to honor (esteem highly) all men. Think how this command condemns much of man's treatment of his fellow man today! The violation of this principle has contributed tremendously to the great social evils that prevail in the world, such as war, racism, oppression, exploitation, slavery, abortion, communism, pornography, and the like. Men should be honored because (1) they are in the image of God even though that image is marred by the fall (Gen. 9:6) and (2) it is commanded by God. One doesn't have to read very widely today to find that one of the core reasons why many moderns feel so free to murder babies in the womb or consign men to the *gulag* is that they no longer see man as unique, a moral and accountable being destined to live in a future world of joy or misery. If God is dead or if man is not in the image of God, then all is permitted.

Next Peter commands us to love the brotherhood. Note that it is not just the brothers but the brotherhood — that is, the church — that we are to love. Christ has formed us into a fellowship, or body, with the purpose of united worship of God and the spread of his kingdom. He did not intend us to be Christians in isolation, and so we show love to the church first by joining a local body. (As soon as Paul came to Jerusalem he assayed to join himself to the disciples.) Then we should faithfully support the worship and work there, giving of our time, abilities and resources (cf Acts 4:32ff) and developing and using our spiritual gifts for the benefit of the body. We love the church by seeking to preserve its purity and peace, by helping it to increase in quality and quantity and by praying for it.

At the same time we are to remember that our local church is but a small part of the universal brotherhood of all true believers, which we are to love too. As the Westminster Confession of Faith says:

> Saints by profession are bound to maintain an holy fellowship and communion in the worship of God, and in performing such other spiritual services as tend to their mutual edification; as also in relieving each other in outward things . . . Which communion, as God offereth opportunity, is to be extended to all those who, in every place, call upon the name of the Lord Jesus (Chapter XXVI, "Of the Communion of Saints," Sec. II).

Another duty Peter urges is that of fearing God. This is a reverent awe and holy fear of offending him. When we consider what God is like and what he has said he will do to those who oppose him, certainly it is folly not to fear him (Matt. 10:28). We further this spirit in our lives as we contemplate the divine character as portrayed in Scripture.

Finally we are to honor the king. We are to pay a proper respect to every person who is invested with civil authority, especially those at the head of the government.

Are You Free?

What kind of freedom are you experiencing? the freedom of doing your own thing, throwing off restraints, disregarding proper authority? or the freedom of living morally by God's laws, in the power of his Spirit abstaining from fleshly lusts and actively pursuing good? Has yours been a desire-oriented or commandment-oriented life-style?

Have you been submitting to proper authority? Is there any area where you are violating the civil law — taxes or speed limits, for instance?

Are you concerned about your Christian testimony — how your behavior commends or detracts from the promotion of Christ's cause?

Are you honoring all men—even those still needing the Savior and desired by Christ — viewing them as God's image-bearers and not to be mistreated or demeaned?

Do you love the brotherhood? Are you a truly supportive member of a local church? Do you love the broader fellowship of Christ's body, even those whose theology and practice, while sufficiently orthodox to be Christian, still differ considerably from yours? Do you see the gap as being between the church and the world or between one section of the church and another?

Brother, are *you* free?

Review Questions

1. Why should Christians be concerned to obey the civil authority?
2. For what purpose does God ordain human government?
3. When, if ever, could a Christian be justified in resisting or even seeking to overthrow the government?
4. How can we effectively abstain from fleshly lusts?
5. Describe Christian freedom.

Discussion Questions

1. What are some common ways Christians tend to disregard the civil law today?

2. Breakdown in law and order is one of the biggest problems in our society. What do you believe to be some of the contributing causes? How can we help remedy the situation?
3. What are some abuses of Christian freedom that you have encountered or even found yourself practicing?
4. What the Christian experiences as freedom because he now desires to do God's will, the nonchristian views as slavery. Realizing that God must open his mind, how can we best overcome his false perspective?
5. What are some ways our local churches could better fulfill the command to love the brotherhood in the sense of the broader body?

6

IT DOESN'T SEEM FAIR

1 Peter 2:18-25

How should a Christian respond when he is treated unfairly? That's an important question since it is a common occurrence for all of us, and most of us don't handle it very well. A lot of people short-circuit their spiritual fruitfulness because of bitterness, anger, unforgiving attitudes and a wide assortment of the works of the flesh. Conversely, if we can handle it correctly it can contribute dramatically to our Christian growth. I heard a leader of an international Christian organization tell of first beginning to experience the fullness of God's Spirit in his life when he followed Peter's principles for handling unfair treatment.

Submit to Unjust Treatment? (2:18-21)

Peter had been speaking of submission to civil authority. Now he exhorts Christians to handle unjust treatment in the same way — by submitting to it (vss 18-20). In the context he is specifically addressing slaves, but the principle applies broadly to other relationships. The Greek for *masters* is *despotai*, a strong word denoting absolute ownership and uncontrolled power. All of us have masters to some degree whether in the business world, at home, in school or in church. Peter speaks of two kinds of masters — the considerate, fair ones and the cruel, unfair ones. Peter encourages uncomplaining persistence in submission even when it involves the painful endurance of unjust treatment. Don't we have a right to retaliation or rebellion when we're treated unfairly? Says Peter, no!

The reasons he gives are that this is pleasing to God and a part of our calling. God is pleased when we patiently submit to unjust treatment when we have done nothing to deserve it. Such submission to suffering when we have done wrong is to be expected and deserves no special praise, but submission when we have done well does deserve such. The great principle Peter wants us to act from is conscience toward God—we submit to unfair treatment without retaliation because *God* would have us do this.

The Christian believes that his present circumstances are controlled by the providence of God. He knows God will support him in this situation and is using it for his good. Moreover Christians are called to this type of behavior (vs 21). *Calling* here refers to the divine call in Christ to become members of his people. Also this is a calling to become Christlike — conformed to his image — and *he* submitted to unjust suffering. God uses such unjust sufferings to mold our character.

How Did Christ Handle Mistreatment? (2:21-25)

Peter says that Christ is our example in submitting to mistreatment (vs 21). His suffering was for us and his manner of bearing it provides us an example as we seek to follow his steps. Peter details Christ's mistreatment: he was totally innocent, without sin or deceitful talk (vs 22; cf Is. 53:9). Yet he was reviled and he suffered—think of the buffeting, the crown of thorns, the scourging and finally the crucifixion (vs 23). How would you have responded to such treatment? Historians tell us that men being crucified usually cursed and spat upon those around them. Jesus' behavior? He submitted to it in patient endurance. When he was reviled he didn't respond in like manner or resort to threats. He even prayed for his enemies!

He also entrusted himself to God. The Greek literally says "he handed himself over" to God — the same word used of his being handed over to wicked men in his betrayal. He commits himself and his cause to God's hands (cf 4:19). He believed that in due time God as a righteous judge would vindicate him. Of course, God did so when he raised him from the dead and seated him at his own right hand.

Here then is our example. When we're treated unfairly, remember how Jesus responded and that we're called to do likewise, submit patiently to it and hand ourselves and our case over to God. This doesn't mean that we should never defend ourselves, but we should be very careful that our spirit in such situations is like Christ's and not like the world's.

Having touched on Christ's suffering Peter goes on to speak of the nature and purpose of Christ's death (vs 24). Its nature was that of a substitutionary atonement: he bore our sins (cf Is. 53:12). An event from American history may help us understand. In an Indian tribe chickens began to disappear. Someone was stealing them. This was a serious matter and the chief decreed that the thief when caught would receive ten lashes. When the stealing continued he raised it to twenty lashes and finally to one hundred, which would very possibly mean death for the thief. Then it was discovered that the thief was the chief's elderly mother. The tribe wondered whether justice would be set aside by the chief. To their amazement, on the appointed day he gave instructions for her to be bound to the whipping post. He placed the whip in a young brave's hand and said, "One hundred lashes!" But then he took off his shirt and wrapped his own body around his mother's, himself taking the blows that should have fallen on her. That's what Jesus did for us!

The purpose of this suffering, however, was not only to atone for our sin but to destroy the dominion of sin in all who come to him, so that we might die to sin and live unto righteousness. Christ died to make us into godly men and women. Dying to sin is something we must do daily and moment by moment, but because of the power of God's Spirit the Christian can progressively do this. And each case of mistreatment is a fresh revelation of how we are doing in this area and a fresh opportunity to practice the principle of submission and die to sin.

The reference to stripes is a quote from Isaiah 53, from which Peter has been drawing (vs 25). Sin is often represented in Scripture as a disease. Through Christ's death and our repentance and faith there is healing.

Peter reminds them of the great healing that has occurred in their lives: they were lost sheep, but now they have a Shepherd and Bishop for their souls. In repentance and faith they have returned from their wandering.

> I was a wand'ring sheep, I would not be controlled;
> But now I love my Shepherd's voice, I love, I love the fold.

I was a wayward child, I once preferred to roam;
But now I love my Father's voice, I love, I love his home.

—Horatius Bonar

Putting It into Practice

Christians need not wonder and shouldn't be discouraged when they meet with unfair treatment. It is part of our calling and an opportunity to put these principles into practice and grow spiritually.

We need to be careful that our suffering is not due to our own folly or sin. Not every sufferer has fellowship with Christ in his sufferings—we are not like him if we bring it upon ourselves.

Even if you were the best man in the world, though you suffered to the greatest degree you would be suffering far less than you deserve. All suffering is ultimately by the will of God. Some suffering is deserved—God's punishment. Some is undeserved and yet is for God's glory as we share in Christ's suffering. However unjust it is when it comes from man, coming from God it is just; and we should see in the men of the world who mistreat us the hand of God.

If Christ died to secure our death to sin and bring us unto righteousness, shouldn't that motivate us to follow his example in patient suffering? What are our sufferings compared to his? Is there someone you are bitter toward and need to forgive? Have you been defending yourself instead of committing your case to God?

Have you experienced the kind of change Peter described? Have you returned to the Shepherd and Bishop of your soul?

Review Questions

1. What is the basic response Peter calls for when we experience unfair treatment?
2. What reasons does Peter give as to why we should respond in this fashion?
3. What does undeserved suffering do for us?
4. How did Christ respond to unjust treatment?
5. What was the nature and purpose of Christ's death?

Discussion Questions

1. What happens in our relation to the Lord when we don't submit in our relation to man?
2. What times can you think of where it would be proper not to submit to mistreatment?
3. Do you know anyone who has practiced this patient endurance of mistreatment? What was the effect?
4. What to you is the most difficult thing about practicing this principle? What is the strongest motive for doing it?

7

ISN'T MY HOME MY CASTLE?

1 Peter 3:1-7

How to relate to your mate is one of the crucial areas of our day. The family is in disarray. Sixty percent of women in their thirties will be divorced. More than one-third of all children born in the 1970s will have spent part of their childhood living with a single parent. Christian homes are by no means immune to this. One couple put on their wedding invitation, "We know God has intended us for each other." But as someone said, God must have changed his mind, because they were divorced within a year.

The causes of the breakdown most often cited are incompatibility and infidelity. Someone has labeled the first "The Myth of Incompatibility," because we are all incompatible! The basic problem in marriage is selfishness, and we are all selfish. Dr. Larry Crabb, in a conference I attended, referred to the *unspoken* vows that are in the hearts of those participating in the marriage ceremony: "You really meet my needs. As a matter of fact, you do such a good job of it that I'm going to give you the opportunity to do that on a fuller, long-range basis." You can see the coming collision since only Christ can meet a number of our needs and since our goal should be to love the other person—that is, meet his or her needs.

The goal of having my needs met is that of a parasite, like a tick feeding on a dog. The problem, as Dr. Crabb pointed out, is that in the typical marriage you have two ticks and no dog! As you can see, while the subject of this section of our study is the husband-and-wife relationship, the principles are of broad application and touch us all whatever our marital status. It is interesting to see how Peter approaches the subject. Today so much attention is put on an individual's *rights*, but Peter talks of the *duties* of each party.

Submit? to *Him?* (3:1-6)

The instruction to wives is to submit to their husbands (vs 1). This is the scriptural teaching wherever one looks in the Bible. Some say that the emphasis on wives obeying was due to the particular culture, and if the apostles were writing today they would talk more of equality. But Paul, in a similar passage (Eph. 5:22-33), does not base his instruction on culture but on God's order of creation: "For the husband is the head of the wife, even as Christ is the head of the church." By her obedience the wife shows her respect for the divine ordering of human relationships.

This does not imply inferiority. The subordination is one of function. Christ wasn't inferior when he became obedient to his Father. He did so to fulfill the function of Mediator. Every team needs a head.

We see the *principle* of submission—note the parallel to other human relations: Peter says, "*Likewise,* ye wives, be in subjection." This principle of submission to proper authority has already been discussed in relation to how the Christian was to respond to civil authority, and the slave to his master even if he was unfair. A wife is to submit in a similar way. This does not mean she shouldn't be free to express her opinions and desires, but when there is a disagreement and the husband feels they must go in a particular direction, she is to accept his decision. Of course, as we saw before, there is a limit—she is not to participate in anything sinful if so directed.

Having issued the call to submission, Peter covers the case of the unbelieving husband. Many Christian wives are in this situation, though a Christian is told to marry "only in the Lord" (1 Cor. 7:39). The wife may have disobeyed God in entering such a marriage or she may have been deceived, thinking him a Christian; or she may have become a Christian after getting married.

The husband is described as not obeying the word. The implication seems to be that of active hostility. Great questions and struggles often arise in the wife's heart in such a position. I recently received a letter from one full of questions:

> I don't think I have any biblical out—do you?
>
> When is my anger toward my husband justified—ever??
>
> Where is God when I feel so alone, so afraid, so powerless?
>
> I feel defeated—WHERE'S THE POWER?
>
> Must I love my husband? how? respect him? honor him?
>
> What do those things boil down to in everyday give-and-take situations?
>
> Is love something you do or something I really feel if I'm spiritually right?

The goal, of course, is to *win* that unbelieving spouse to Christ. The term is a military one—she is to seek to take him captive for Christ!

The approach Peter advocates is to do this without the word, by her behavior. She gives her witness not by preaching at him but by living before him. Her chaste conversation (manner of life) coupled with fear will be observed attentively by her husband and will make an impact on him. *Chaste* implies the avoidance of everything inconsistent with purity of mind and life; *fear* refers to the fear of God or reverence for his authority.

As a pastor I have often talked to unbelieving husbands of Christian wives about their need of Christ. Where the wife has done as Peter says, a strong platform is provided for the penetration of the gospel. Peter isn't saying the wife should *never* share the gospel with her unbelieving husband. But she should not be constantly dragging him to meetings, getting him to listen to TV ministers or tapes, and so on.

Peter urges the cultivation of true beauty (vss 3, 4). When he says her adorning shouldn't be outward—the plaiting of the hair and the wearing of gold—he is not prohibiting all jewelry or an attractive hair style. (Note the reference to the putting on of apparel—surely he is not absolutely forbidding that!) Sarah is mentioned (vs 6) as a godly woman; and while no reference is made to her wearing jewelry, when Abraham sent his servant to find a bride for Isaac the servant took gold bracelets and earrings (Gen. 24:22f). What is forbidden is dependence on excessive jewelry or an undue expense on outward appearance. Such breeds pride, is poor stewardship and displays wrong values.

Rather the beauty she should cultivate is that of the hidden man of the heart — a gentle and imperturbable spirit. *Meek* describes among other things the way she submits to her husband. The opposite is a domineering and discontented spirit. As Proverbs 27:15 says, "A continual dropping in a very rainy day and a contentious woman are alike." Similarly 21:19: "It is better to dwell in the wilderness, than with a contentious and an angry woman." She is to develop her Christian character. This is in the sight of God of great price. She values the things praised by God rather than those praised by man. These spiritual values are not corruptible like earthly treasure.

Note the person's awareness that God's eye is upon him or her and his understanding that what is valued in God's sight should determine how he acts.

Peter, having urged the cultivation of true beauty, has a comparison with godly women of the Old Testament (vss 5, 6). They adorned themselves in this same manner — their lives were adorned by those desirable characteristics of personal conduct, especially submission to their husbands. Sarah is cited as an illustration of such, both in her obeying Abraham and her referring to him as "lord" (cf Gen. 18:12).

Christian women should want to be spiritual daughters of Sarah and are such when their behavior is like hers. As Abraham is father of the faithful so Sarah is mother of the obedient. The phrase *as long as you are . . . not afraid with any amazement* (Gk. *ptoesis,* "terror") probably means that godly women are composed, having a spirit of quiet confidence rather than fear or alarm.

Honor *Her?* as the Weaker *What?* (3:7)

Peter's instruction to the husband is a call to considerateness. Husbands should dwell with them according to knowledge (NIV "be considerate") — that is, they should be informed and guided by a proper awareness of their wives' needs and nature. That is no small order.

It was some years before I even began to understand my wife's needs, much less was able to meet them. I can't meet *all* of her needs, but one of my major goals in life is to meet all I can. That attitude is crucial. It is the essence of Christian love — to give of one's self for the welfare of the other. While both parties are to love each other, the basic assignment to husbands is to love their wives, even as Christ also loved the church and gave himself for it (Eph. 5:25). That's quite a standard of love!

Husbands are to give honor unto the wife as unto the weaker vessel. The Greek for *honor* is used to describe a great treasure. He should recognize her more limited power and give corresponding considerateness.

In other words treat her as a treasure, a precious vase, not as a washbucket. For many years I was inconsiderate of my wife, never helping with her work load and not supporting her emotionally. When the going was rough I expected her to "suck it up," as the saying goes.

The husband also is to regard his wife as an heir with him of the grace of life. He should view her spiritually as a fellow sharer in the grace of God and in his gift to both of them — life and eternal life. He should understand that their union is to be a spiritual partnership bearing fruit to

God. I am convinced that my wife and I are much more effective for Christ as a team than we could be individually.

Peter warns of the consequence to their spiritual lives if these principles aren't applied. Do this, he says, that your prayers be not hindered. Disharmony in the home often results in resentments and hurtful actions, and these hinder our walk with God. "If I regard iniquity in my heart, the Lord will not hear me" (Ps. 66:18). So it is crucial that we guard against anything that damages our relationship with each other.

My Home, My Castle?

As we can see, the home is not so much a castle where others wait on us but a crucible where a lot of grinding is applied to our egos, to teach us to die to self and learn to practice real love for others. If we can learn these lessons there we can practice them anywhere, since home seems to be the hardest place to practice submissiveness, considerateness and the other principles discussed.

If you are married, how is it in your relation with your spouse? Have you been complaining, "I am not getting what I want out of marriage" instead of thinking of what you vowed to *give* in the marriage? Are you obeying God's instruction to you in your position? We must not wait until the other person starts obeying God's instruction: we must start with ourselves. We need daily to focus on how we're measuring up to God's will—not how the other person is doing.

I recently counseled with a couple who were on the verge of divorce. They were focusing on their needs and each other's failures. Between the first two counseling sessions she told him to bring home the divorce papers for her to sign. But then they did two things. First, they started studying the Bible together using a simple method recommended by Charlie Shedd. He suggested marking a passage with a candle to indicate insight, a question mark to indicate puzzlement and an arrow to indicate something that applied personally. They did this separately, then discussed their findings and prayed together. They found this very helpful.

Second, they began to try to meet the other's needs and to test themselves by the biblical instructions on the role of each in marriage. This isn't easy, because habits are hard to break; but the progress has been amazing! Let me challenge you to go and do likewise.

Of course the principles apply to situations other than marriage. Think through how they apply at the office (is there someone whose needs you can meet?) or on the team or in your group. God wants to make a difference *through* us, but first he has to do it *in* us.

Review Questions

1. Is the pattern Peter outlines meant for us today?
2. Suppose the husband isn't reasonable or understanding or is not a Christian; is the wife still to submit?
3. What is the basic problem in most marriages?
4. How should a Christian wife seek to win her unbelieving husband to Christ?

5. What are some ways in which a husband can honor his wife?

Discussion Questions

1. If you are or have been married, were there unspoken vows when you got married?
2. How would you answer the questions asked by the lady who was married to an unbeliever?
3. Do you know anyone who was won by an unbelieving spouse? What method did the spouse use?
4. How does it affect your spiritual life when there is disharmony between you and your spouse?
5. What application can you see of these principles outside marriage?

8

WHY NOT GET EVEN?

1 Peter 3:8-12

"Don't get mad, get even!" How often have you heard that? One of the earliest chapters of the Bible describes man's tendency to want to get even:

> And Lamech said unto his wives . . . If Cain shall be avenged sevenfold, truly Lamech seventy and sevenfold (Gen. 4:23, 24).

Certainly we all know that urge and on occasion have indulged it. Peter addresses that tendency as he continues unfolding tenets of Christian living in relation to one's fellowman. First he speaks of how to act toward fellow Christians, and then how to act toward those who wrong you.

How to Act toward Fellow Christians (3:8)

Peter mentions five very important duties in our relation with fellow Christians. We are to *be of one mind*. Actually we are to "mind the same things." The idea is to be united by a common interest and outlook (NIV "live in harmony with one another"). This is a recurring and strong appeal throughout the New Testament. Christ prayed that all who would believe in him would be one as he and his Father are one (John 17:20, 21). Paul wrote to the Philippians, "[S]tand fast in one spirit, with one mind . . . [B]e like-minded, having the same love, being of one accord, of one mind" (Phil. 1:27, 2:2; cf Eph. 4:13-15).

This doesn't mean that Christians have to think alike on everything, but it does mean to be united on the essentials of Christianity in both our faith and practice. We might say, "But how can we have the same mind? Those who profess to be Christians differ sharply even on issues like abortion." Only as we have a mind informed by and *subject to* the word of God can we be of one mind.

We must not insist on a greater extent of union than the things that are clearly revealed in Scripture. Some insist that we be of the same mind in points not so clearly revealed or on inferences drawn from biblical teaching. Such insistence creates division. When we strive with each other instead of striving together it is a real stumbling block to others.

I will never forget my first presbytery meeting. Two of the most prominent ministers there engaged in a shouting match. I was in shock — think how such affects the non-christian viewer! It was when the early church was of one heart and of one soul that great grace was upon them all (Acts 4:32, 33).

We are to *be sympathetic* with one another. The King James Version says "having compassion," but the Greek *sumpatheis* ("suffering together") is the root of our word *sympathy*. It means to have responsive fellow feeling for others — rejoicing with those who rejoice and weeping with those who weep (Rom. 12:15). A little girl said to her mother, "Sally was crying because her cat got run over by a car, but I helped her." "How did you help her?" "I cried too."

There is something very important in that little story. A young couple in my congregation had a baby stillborn. Later they commented that, of all those who came to see them, I was the most comfort. It wasn't anything I said, it was the fact that I cried with them. I wonder how many times I've failed to comfort because I didn't truly weep with them.

Sometimes God uniquely equips us to sympathize through difficult things we've experienced. Another couple in my church had a teenage daughter killed in an automobile accident. Many sought to give sympathy, but the only couple who were really able to communicate that sympathy effectively had lost a daughter in a similar way.

We are to *be loving*. Peter's urging to love as brethren (Gk. *philadelphoi*) means to love one another because we are now brothers, members of the same family of God. Brotherly love is the badge of Christian discipleship (John 13:35). John says anyone who does not love his brother has not passed from death to life (1 John 3:14).

A member of my congregation asked me whether he should sue a Christian friend who had cheated him out of ten thousand dollars. Such questions usually don't have simple answers, but as we wrestled with brother going to law with brother (1 Cor. 6:6) I said, "If he were your physical brother, would you sue him?" Immediately he responded, "No!" And that settled his course of action.

The verses that teach the necessity of loving our brother are as true as the ones that teach the necessity of faith in Christ, but I wonder if they hold the same place of importance in our churches.

I sometimes ask students being examined for ordination, "Which is the more biblical church—one where doctrinal views are correct and there is little love, or one where the doctrinal system, while adhering to the essentials, is still very weak, but there is a real love manifest?" Of course neither is truly biblical, but too often we are willing to settle for one or the other.

Such love should generate much forbearance and sacrifice. John says, "Hereby perceive we the love of God, because he laid down his life for us: and we ought to lay down our lives for the brethren" (1 John 3:16). If I ought to be willing to lay down my life for my Christian brother I certainly ought to be willing to show love in many important ways that are less demanding. This Christian brother may not be of my theological, political or economic persuasion, yet I am to show love in very practical ways.

We are to *be compassionate* (NIV; KJV "pitiful"; RV "tenderhearted"). The word means "quick to feel and show affection." We are to cherish kind feelings toward those in distress. It is easy to become callous when we are constantly confronted by people in need, and we must fight the tendency. I heard of a beggar who knocked on the door of a tavern and asked if he might have a meal. The lady who answered roundly rebuked him as a shiftless bum and slammed the door. He started to leave and then looked at the name of the tavern — St. George and the

Dragon—and knocked again. When she answered he said, "Please, may I speak to St. George this time?"

A lady in our church periodically will say, "You've got to see something!" She will take me to a poor home where the conditions are awful and say, "We must do something!" She is right and she is practicing compassion. This compassion looks at both soul and body needs and seeks to meet both, but knows there is no poverty like soul poverty. Jesus shows such compassion will evidence the reality of our faith in the final judgment.

> Come, ye blessed . . . inherit the kingdom . . . For I was an hungred, and ye gave me meat . . . Then shall the righteous answer . . . when saw we thee an hungred, and fed thee? . . . Inasmuch as ye have done it unto one of the least of these my brethren, ye have done it unto me (Matt. 25:34-40).

Finally we are to *be humble* (NIV; the KJV "be courteous" is translating a different Greek word but most authorities follow the NIV rendering.) Humility was looked at by the Greeks as a sign of weakness, but Christ was meek and lowly of heart and calls us to be like him. Most of the division among Christians is due to a lack of humility.

> He humbled Himself to the manger,
> And even to Calvary's tree;
> But I am so proud and unwilling,
> His humble disciple to be.

How to Act toward Those Who Wrong You (3:9-12)

Peter now indicates how Christians should act toward those who purposely hurt and persecute them. How to behave in such circumstances is a theme he often refers to throughout the book.

First he indicates negatively *what not to do* (vs 9). The natural response is to render evil for evil, but Peter says we should not seek to get even. Jesus taught that if someone smites us on the right cheek, instead of striking back we are to offer him the left (Matt. 5:39). I read of a well-known fighter who became a Christian. An enemy thinking to take advantage of his professed conversion mocked his Christianity rudely and then struck him on the right side of his jaw. The fighter shook his head and then thoughtfully offered the left side, which his opponent promptly struck. The new convert proceeded to roll up his sleeves and with the remark, "That's all the instructions I received from my Master," waded into his antagonist. Of course what Jesus and Peter are seeking to restrain is the spirit of retaliation. At the same time this should not be understood as an absolute forbidding of self defense or even of calling a persecutor to account. When Paul and Silas were unlawfully beaten and imprisoned they required the guilty officials to come personally and escort them out (Acts 16:37).

Getting rid of the spirit of retaliation is critical and challenging. Early in my ministry I wrote an article in a local newspaper about the infiltration of communism into some of the upper levels of church hierarchy. A local minister wrote an answering article. I answered his article and he mine, and then I prepared one that was going to blast him out of the water! At this point I became convicted about the sinfulness of my spirit of retaliation. One of the hardest things I've ever done, and yet one of the most significant for my spiritual growth, was to tear up that article.

Peter next says positively *what to do*. Instead of railing we are to bless those who hurt us (cf Matt. 5:44; 1 Cor. 4:12). The Greek *eulogein*, from which our word *eulogize* comes, includes the concept of speaking well of, showing active kindness toward, and praying God's blessing upon them. We should speak to them courteously and, as far as truth permits, speak well of them. We don't have to approve what they do, but we do need to desire their true welfare.

Why should we do these things? Peter gives his reasons.

First, it is a *part of our calling* (vs 9). Such behavior, in direct contrast to our natural propensity, is the kind of behavior to which Christ calls us. We are to be like Christ (2:21) and like our heavenly Father (Matt. 5:44, 45).

Second, it will cause us to *inherit a blessing*. If we truly want God to bless us this is an important condition to fulfill. The blessing is both in this life and in the next.

In verses 10-12 Peter confirms with Scripture the fact that this is the path of blessing as he quotes Psalm 34:12-16. The reference states what we are to do in order to see good days (have true enjoyment of life).

First, we must control our tongues, giving up hurtful and deceitful words. The admonition to refrain from such indicates the struggle necessary. James warns us of the tongue: "a restless evil, full of deadly poison" (3:8, NIV). A friend of mine who is an excellent golfer was recently playing with a fellow golfer whose tongue was anything but restrained. After one oath my soft-spoken friend said, "You just cursed the only Being in the universe who could have helped your golf game." He is also the only one who can enable us to control our tongues!

Second, we must do good and not evil (vs 11). This is a deliberate and daily choice on our part.

Third, we must seek peace. The same verse pictures a vigorous pursuit of peace with others. Jesus said, "Blessed are the peacemakers" (Matt. 5:9).

The psalmist goes on to indicate that God will defend the righteous and deal with those that do evil (vs 12). His eyes are on the righteous—this refers to his omniscience, providence and favor. He is not unmindful of or indifferent to the injustices they experience; and his ears are open or attentive to their prayers. We must remember that there is none righteous as to our having kept God's law, but that he accounts us righteous when we put our trust in Christ as the one who paid for our unrighteousness. There is also an imparted righteousness or corresponding progressive change in our behavior.

God's face is against them that do evil. The face of God is always a matter of awe and fear in the Old Testament (cf Ex. 33:20). One implication seems to be that we need not be concerned to get even, for "Vengeance is mine; I will repay, saith the Lord" (Rom. 12:19).

How Actively Are We Applying These Principles?

Examine your life. Is there someone toward whom you need to make a change in your behavior? Are there some fellow Christians with whom you need to be of one mind? Is there a Christian brother toward whom you need to manifest love instead of cutting him down behind his back? Are you becoming like the dragon instead of St. George in the area of compassion? Have you felt justified in getting even with those who have mistreated you?

Several years ago I heard a speaker who challenged the audience to pick several people they didn't like and begin praying for them and seeking to do good to them. I picked two men, both fellow ministers, and began praying for them, asking God to bless them and show me ways to do good to them. To my utter amazement, one called me after a few months and asked me to preach at a conference for his church. I accepted and sought to do it in a manner that would be acceptable to him. We have since had the opportunity of helping each other in a number of ways and have become close friends. I haven't had any contact with the other man but am still praying for him. Is there someone you need to start blessing today?

Review Questions

1. How can Christians be of one mind when often there is sharp division on issues like abortion or national defense?
2. Which is more critical in a congregation, correct doctrinal views or the manifestation of brotherly love?
3. Does the admonition not to render evil for evil forbid self-defense or calling the persecutor to account?
4. What is involved in blessing those who hurt us?
5. What reasons does Peter give as to why we should refrain from getting even and rather bless those who mistreat us?

Discussion Questions

1. What benefit is to be gained from our being mistreated by others?
2. Have you had an experience of someone sympathizing with you or showing compassion when it really made a significant difference?
3. Have you found yourself becoming calloused and insensitive and then discovered something that helped in combating that tendency?
4. It is natural to feel that if I don't get even the other party will continue to abuse me. How would you counsel someone wrestling with that?
5. How important to our spiritual growth is the overcoming of a spirit of retaliation?

9

"I NEVER KNOW WHAT TO SAY"

1 Peter 3:13-22

When I became a Christian I was already in seminary and was pastoring a church on weekends. I immediately had a deep desire to learn to share the gospel in personal conversation with others, since I was conscious of how easy it is to miss the way. I decided to practice on hitch-hikers I'd pick up *en route* to the church. I'd start talking about Christ and pretty soon the hitchhiker would say, "Let me out!" So I'd let him out and get me another one! Upon graduation I started a new church and sought to make personal evangelism very much a part of our approach to ministry as a church. I soon discovered that it was a very controversial thing in a community when a top businessman or a judge or a publisher became converted and began sharing his faith. Peter writes to Christians who also are in the midst of swirling controversy, giving direction to them on how to conduct themselves.

Apologize for Our Faith? (3:13-17)

Peter continues to write about the proper response to persecution.

First he discusses the *result of persecution* (vss 13, 14). He says that for Christians who live as they ought (NIV "eager to do good") the probability of suffering is small. But if you are persecuted for righteousness' sake, happy are you.

For righteousness' sake could cover anything from spreading the gospel to exposing immoral or unjust practices in society. You are happy (NIV "blessed") because it is a privilege to suffer for Christ's sake (Phil. 1:29) and because God causes all things to work together for good to those who love him (Rom. 8:28). Human adversities are God's universities through which God grows us up.

Peter, in speaking of their *response to persecution* (vss 14-17), indicates what not to do and then what to do. He says, "[B]e not afraid of their terror, neither be troubled"—don't fear their threats. It is hard not to be afraid, especially when there is the threat of loss of property, reputation, job, friends or even life. Think of Peter's fear which caused him to deny Christ three times! Even the "fear of the sneer" can sometimes paralyze us from witnessing.

An answer to this fear and the response Peter calls for is to sanctify Christ as Lord in your heart (vs 15, RV). Peter is alluding to Isaiah 8:12-14 where Isaiah counsels not to fear Assyria: "Sanctify the LORD of hosts himself, and let him be your fear . . . And he shall be for a sanctuary." Guard against the fear of man by cultivating the proper fear of God. To sanctify Christ as Lord means to reverence him as Lord, realizing that he is in control, seeing him as governing and protecting his own.

I have a little poem I repeat when I face a difficult witnessing situation:

> Not me the dark foe fears at all,
> But hid in Thee I take the field;
> And at my feet the mighty fall,
> For Thou hast bid them yield.

The dark foe is Satan and he that is in you is greater than he that is in the world.

Peter continues, "[B]e ready always to give an answer to every man that asketh you a reason of the hope that is in you." The Greek word for "answer" is *apologia,* meaning "an apology" or speech in defense. From this we have the discipline of apologetics, which marshals the evidences for the truth of Christianity. We are to be ready—prepared at all times—to give a reason (Gk. *logos*) or logical explanation of the hope that is distinctive of the Christian.

We have already discussed our confident expectation of persevering and going to heaven. We are to do this in meekness and fear (NIV "with gentleness and respect").

How can we learn to do this? There are so many hard questions critics can throw at us! Actually there are less than a dozen really common objections to Christianity, and with a little study we can learn to handle these reasonably well. There are many excellent books that can help us with this, such as Paul Little's *How to Give Away Your Faith,* R. C. Sproul's *A Reason to Believe,* D. James Kennedy's *Why I Believe,* C. S. Lewis's *Mere Christianity* and Josh Mc-Dowell's *Evidence That Demands a Verdict.* I recall a doctor I talked with who raised many of the common objections covered in these books. I was able to give biblical answers and after several months of such discussions he committed his life to Christ, saying that for the first time someone had not sidestepped the questions. This is the type of thing to which Peter is referring. "The heart of the righteous studieth to answer" (Prov. 15:28).

We should also be able to give a clear and convincing personal testimony of what Christ has done in our lives. Go through the book of Acts and notice how often Paul uses this approach.

In responding to persecution we should maintain a good conscience (vs 16). A good conscience is one that approves rather than condemns one's own actions and attitudes. Our witness is to be coupled with a good conscience that grows out of good behavior. By this conscientious and consistent conduct detractors will be put to shame. On the other hand, one unchristian action on our part will cast more discredit on Christianity than our most eloquent apologetic can offset.

Peter sums this up by again relating our suffering to God's will (vs 17), indicating that there is purpose in it and profit should come out of it. It might be helpful to distinguish between God's preceptive will (his precepts or commands are what he tells us to do) and his planned will (what he has planned to do). The first is often referred to as his revealed will and the second as his secret will, known only to him. The persecutors were violating God's revealed will and thus doing evil; nonetheless the trial was a part of God's plan. Such thinking brings Peter back in thought to the supreme example of such suffering.

The Just for the Unjust? (3:18)

Peter now gives *the reason for Christ's sufferings*. He details the nature of Christ's sufferings: he was undergoing the punishment for sins as our substitute, the just for (Gk. *huper*, "on behalf of") the unjust. Centuries before, Isaiah had prophesied of him: "All we like sheep have gone astray;

we have turned every one to his own way; and the LORD hath laid on him the iniquity of us all."

> The Eternal life, His Life down laid,
> Such was the wondrous plan;
> And God, the blessed God, was made
> A curse for cursed man.

Christ did this once (Gk. *hapax*, "once for all"; cf Heb. 9:28). It did not have to be repeated like the animal sacrifices. Such a concept of a substitutionary atonement has always seemed inconceivable to men who are uncomfortable with such ideas as God's wrath and eternal punishment. I'm reminded of the picture of an old Scottish Covenanter speaking to his daughter:

> There's nae Gospel noo, lassie,
> There's nae Covenant blood,
> There's nae altar noo, lassie,
> There's nae Lamb o' God.
>
> Folks dinna want the cross, lassie,
> They've cutten doon the tree,
> And naebody believe in't,
> But fules like you and me!

The consummation Christ had in view was to bring us to God, says Peter. This is the ultimate goal of Christianity: to reconcile sinners to God, bringing us into his favor and the enjoyment of his presence now, and ultimately the sharing of his glory in the world to come.

The Harrowing of Hell? (3:18-20)

Peter now speaks of *the action of the Spirit in Christ's resurrection and preaching*. This passage is one of the most disputed in the Bible. It speaks of Christ preaching "unto the spirits in prison." Some have taken this to teach that Christ descended to Hades, where Old Testament believers were awaiting his death, and there he proclaimed his atonement. Then he led them to heaven. This has been called the "Harrowing of Hell." To me this view has great difficulties attached. The spirits he preached to are identified as those who were disobedient in Noah's day. Why would he speak only to *this* group? I believe there is a better way of understanding this passage.

The reference to Christ being quickened by the Spirit does not refer to his spirit being made alive after his physical death — his spirit never died. Rather does it refer to his physical resurrection by the Spirit.

Then we have the Spirit's action in Christ's preaching to the spirits in prison (vs 19). These were men who were disobedient to God's revelation in Noah's day (vs 20) and the preaching was done through Noah then. Christ by his Spirit (cf 1:11, Gen. 6:3) called them to repentance through Noah. It was by the Spirit that long ago in Noah's time Christ went and preached to those who are *now* disembodied spirits in prison.

Saved by Baptism? (3:20-22)

The discussion of Noah leads to *a comparison of the salvation of Noah and baptism*. Noah was saved by water. The water that destroyed all the disobedient bore the ark up. Similarly we are saved by baptism, says Peter (vss 21, 22). It is important to look carefully at what Peter means by baptism here. He specifically says he is not referring to external application of water, the putting away of the filth of the flesh, but rather an inner cleansing that brings about a conscience that is freed from the guilt of sin. This is the baptism of the Spirit by which we are placed in Christ (1 Cor. 12:13). By *this* baptism, symbolized by water baptism, we enter Christ as our ark and are saved from judgment.

Peter also brings out the relation to Christ's resurrection and ascension. Being in Christ we are saved by his resurrection—his victory over sin and death. He has ascended and is in the position of authority over all to save all his own.

Laying It to Heart?

Peter has covered a lot in this section that we ought to incorporate into our lives. Are we prepared to give a *reasoned* defense for the hope that is in us? Do we know how to answer the common objections men raise? Why not acquire and study one of the books mentioned? Are we actually witnessing? Are we deterred from a bold stance by the fear of men?

We also need to be prepared to suffer for our faith. Christ calls us to live righteously—proclaiming his lordship and opposing evil. This will on occasion bring persecution and sometimes cost us heavily. Are you currently compromising with your conscience in any area in order to avoid such cost?

It is very important that we have clear views of the nature of Christ's death and stand firmly committed to biblical teaching on this. This is the heart of Christianity and we must not be moved from it!

Let us be sure we are in Christ, the Ark. Has the Spirit so worked in your life that you have repented and placed your faith in Christ? Is your faith bearing fruit?

Review Questions

1. Why does Peter say we are happy (or blessed) if we are persecuted for righteousness sake?
2. What should we do when we find ourselves afraid to stand up for Christ or share our faith?
3. What was the nature of Christ's sufferings?
4. What is meant by Christ "preaching to the spirits in prison"?
5. What does Peter mean when he says, "The like figure whereunto baptism doth also now save us"?

Discussion Questions

1. What is your biggest hindrance in witnessing? What can you do about it?
2. What have you found to be helpful in handling the common objections to the Christian faith?
3. Sometimes the teaching on the atonement described here is referred to as the "satisfaction theory" — just one among other theories. How would you respond to that?
4. The reference to Christ preaching to the spirits in prison is occasionally used to advance the view that there will be a second chance after death to respond to the gospel,

at least for those who never heard the gospel in their life. How would you answer such teaching?

5. Some groups teach that water baptism is essential to salvation and use 1 Peter 3:21 along with Acts 2:38 to support their case. How would you answer them?

10

WHY IS EVERYONE LOOKING AT ME THAT WAY?

1 Peter 4:1-11

When I became a Christian at age twenty-six my immediate thought was, "My old friends don't know the gospel and their lives are very indicative of this. I need to tell them of Christ." So I went back to my hometown and arranged to spend an evening with one of them. Just as I got started telling him, several others dropped in and I decided to tackle all three. But before I could start someone remarked, "We've got enough for poker!" I said, "I don't want to play poker; I want to tell you what Christ has done in my life." Their response was, "We don't want to hear about that. Deal the cards!" They played while I, determined to let them see that I had changed, sat in the corner and read a magazine, feeling very awkward.

Peter speaks in this section of the tensions that arise when our friends don't understand the change that has taken place in our lives.

Be Prepared to Suffer to Do God's Will (4:1-6)

Peter starts with a *challenge* to be willing to suffer in order to obey God (vs 1). As a motive he urges the great fact of Christ's having suffered for us. Dr. Ray Burwick, a member of my congregation, tells of an experience he had in high school. He and a date were attending a Christian gathering. When opportunity was given to testify, he stood up to speak. He had a bad problem with stuttering, but felt sure the Lord would enable him to overcome it since he was speaking for him. Instead he was unable to stop stuttering and was humiliated in front of his girl friend. When he got home he told the Lord in no uncertain terms that this was the last time he'd ever speak up for him. But then it was as if the Lord said, "If I can die for you, can't you stutter for me?"

Peter makes a similar point: that we should apply the cross to our attitudes, cultivating a particular "mind" or mode of thinking whereby we are willing to suffer rather than sin. His statement, "For he that hath suffered . . . hath ceased from sin," is one that is difficult to interpret. Some feel that he is referring to our identification with Christ whereby we are to enter into the consequence of his suffering by faith, reckoning ourselves dead indeed unto sin but alive unto God (Rom. 6:11). If we are united with Christ and he suffered (died) and rose, so did we. The dominion of sin in our lives is broken, and counting that as true can help us part with sin.

I am inclined to believe that he is referring to the purifying effect of physical suffering—affliction humbly borne tends to disengage the heart from sin. Or he is saying that those who have remained faithful to Christ even when it entailed suffering have proved themselves.

Such purification *represented a change* (vs 2). They are no longer to live the rest of their lives "for evil human desires, but rather for the will of God" (NIV). The will of God is found in his word, and it is to be our rule of belief and behavior. Here Peter is saying, Apply the cross to your ambitions. Our ambitions formerly have been set by evil desires, lusts, things that revolved around "me and mine." I recently read the biography of a plastic surgeon who exhibited this change. The crisis came when he started to fill out an insurance form where the question was asked, "Was this surgery necessary or was it only for cosmetic purposes?" He had assured the patient it would be covered and he had often filled out such forms. But now he found he could not lie. He wound up paying the hospital costs himself.

Peter indicates why they should make such a radical change (vs 3). They had "spent enough time in the past doing what pagans choose to do" (NIV). How fruitless that time really was! Thus he calls on us to apply the cross to our actions. However, such a change brings *the consequent misunderstanding* where former associates think it strange when you "run not with them to the same excess of riot" (vs 4). When Augustine was converted to Christ from an immoral life he immediately began avoiding his former mistress. Once he crossed the street to avoid her, but she ran after him saying, "Augustine, it is I, it is I!" "Yes," he said, "but it is not I!"

Such misunderstanding often leads to persecution where former friends speak evil of you (NIV "heap abuse on you"; Gk. *blasphemo*, "to malign or slander"). They don't mind unless you change. You can become religious and they will speak well of you. But if you change, it is convicting and they counterattack. This is painful of course; but we must not let it discourage or deter us from our commitment and we must love them and seek to be winsome. In time I was able to lead a number of my former friends to Christ and now they are officers in my church.

Peter brings in the *coming judgment* wherein those who engage in such persecution will have to give account to God (vs 5). Because of this coming judgment the gospel was preached to the dead, says Peter (vs 6). This is a difficult verse to interpret. Some see this as a preaching done after death, but most commentators follow the concept that they are *now* dead (NIV) but were alive on earth when the preaching of the gospel was done.

Thus the preaching of the gospel not only offers men the benefit of ceasing from sin and being different, it also offers the benefit of escaping judgment. Note that the cross will be the central factor in this judgment. What is our attitude to the one who hung on the cross (who will now be the Judge)? Have we applied the cross to our attitudes, ambitions, actions?

Be Pursuing Loving and Useful Christian Service (4:7-11)

The action called for by Peter is varied and important as he urges six different things to do.

First he calls for *soberness* (vs 7). *Watching* speaks of a state in which all the faculties are awake and active like a sentinel. There is to be a wakeful vigilance for proper opportunities and subjects for prayer and against hindrances. David said, "As for me, I will call upon God; and the LORD shall save me. Evening, and morning, and at noon, will I pray, and cry aloud: and he shall hear my voice" (Ps. 55:16, 17). Peter may have had in mind the way in which, in the Garden of Gethsemane, he went to sleep and failed to watch unto prayer, and then denied Christ. He knew the disastrous results of not heeding this admonition.

Next Peter emphasizes giving priority to the active expression of *fervent love for one another* (vs 8). Christian love is not a warm feeling, it is the determination to place the welfare of others ahead of concern for ourselves. He urges that fervent (NIV "love each other deeply"), intense and continuing love be seen as of first importance—above all things. His reason: because charity (Gk. *agape*, "love") shall cover a multitude of sins. He is not saying that such love merits God's forgiveness of a multitude of our own sins. Rather, here is how love works: it throws a veil over countless sins of another; it is ready to forgive again and again. Peter is referring to Proverbs 10:12, "Hatred stirreth up strifes: but love covereth all sins." A man under the influence of hatred magnifies the offenses of others; one under the influence of love puts down strife, minimizing such offenses. John said, "Beloved, let us love one another: for love is of God; and every one that loveth is born of God, and knoweth God" (1 John 4:7).

One tangible way of manifesting such love is to *show hospitality to one another without grudging* (vs 9). In those days the demands for such hospitality were frequent and heavy and could easily lead to grudging or murmuring. Hospitality in Scripture involved showing kindness to strangers: "Be not forgetful to entertain strangers" (Heb. 13:2). This requires trust in God to provide what is needed. Gaius is singled out by John as a prime example of such hospitality for his housing and helping itinerant evangelists (see 3 John 5-8).

Peter then urged *responsible stewardship* of the varied resources and spiritual gifts God has given to believers (vs 10). "Each one should use whatever spiritual gifts he has received to serve others" (NIV). The phrase *manifold grace of God* (AV) speaks of the wide variety in such spiritual gifts. A spiritual gift is a special ability bestowed by God's Spirit on the believer for service to the body of Christ. Every Christian has received such a gift (or gifts) from God and holds it in trust for the whole church. The ministry of each is to be according to the character of his particular gift.

The main types of ministry are then distinguished: first, ministry by the spoken word (that is, preaching, teaching); second, ministry in acts of practical kindness such as showing hospitality (vs 11).

It is very important to discover, develop and use our spiritual gifts. If we don't do so we will be unfulfilled and the church will not be helped as would otherwise be possible. Some years ago a gentleman joined my church. He was a new convert, and since he had been a world-class athlete I used him to share his testimony on a number of occasions. Then I got him to try small group Bible studies, and then to be part of our personal evangelism program. None of these seemed to be exactly his slot, and he began to drift away from the church and the Lord. One day he came into my office with an advertisement of a Christian conference on the family being held in Kansas City. He said he thought he would attend and see what tools were available to help a local church better support the family. I was thrilled. When he came back all excited we put him in charge of a committee to implement his ideas. He was fulfilled and the whole church was helped. Today he is a leader in our congregation.

Note the attitude throughout this section that the Christian life is to be lived in the light of the impending consummation: "The end . . . is at hand" (vs 7). This perspective is found throughout the epistles; for example, "[T]his . . . is the last hour" (1 John 2:18, NIV); "[E]ncourage one another . . . as you see the Day approaching" (Heb. 10:25, NIV). Some take Peter's reference to the end as referring to the end of Israel as a nation; however, I take it as referring to Christ's return, for which God would have each generation of Christians to be prepared. This awareness should lend a sense of eternal value to daily living (cf 2 Peter 3:9-14).

Peter concludes this section with *the great objective* of all Christian living: that God may be glorified in everything. God is glorious and his glory consists of his attributes, such as his wisdom, power and goodness. He is glorified when men come to know him as he is and give him glory as they worship and serve him. God is glorified in his son Jesus Christ, who is the full revelation of God. Such glorifying of God should be the goal and crowning satisfaction of Christian service.

Be Persevering in Applying These Principles

How much suffering has your walk with Christ entailed? Are you prepared to suffer in order to obey him? How many years have you spent in a life-style that, while fashionable with the world, is contrary to God's word? Surely too much time. Let the rest be spent in wholeheartedly doing God's will!

Has Christ brought a change in your life so that with Augustine you can say, "Yes, but it is not I"? How have you responded when associates have persecuted you for the change? Have you sought to win them?

Are you watching and praying? How does your practice of prayer compare with Peter's emphasis? Why not decide what heeding Peter's admonition would mean for you and resolve right now to practice that?

How are you doing on loving others and covering a multitude of sins? Are you magnifying or minimizing others' offenses?

Do you know your spiritual gift and are you using it for service to God as a good steward? Is your goal to have all things about your life glorify God?

Have you applied the cross to your attitudes, ambitions and actions?

> To every man there openeth
> A Way, and Ways, and a Way.
> And the High Soul climbs the High Way,
> And the Low Soul gropes the Low.
> And in between, on the misty flats,
> The rest drift to and fro.
> But to every man there openeth
> A High Way, and a Low.
> And every man decideth
> The way his soul shall go.
>
> —John Oxenham

Review Questions

1. According to Peter what characterizes the nonchristian life?
2. What can a person expect to happen when he becomes a Christian and his life really changes?

3. What consequence can those who heap abuse on Christians expect?
4. What should characterize the rest of our lives?
5. What should be our primary objective in life?

Discussion Questions

1. Can you think of a time when you suffered in order to cease from sin?
2. Have you experienced the kind of reaction Peter envisions of people thinking it strange that you don't "run to the same excess of riot" with them?
3. Before you became a Christian did you have occasion to see someone's life dramatically change through Christ? How did you react?
4. What do you find to be most difficult in watching unto prayer? most helpful?
5. What do you believe your spiritual gift is? How did you discover it?

11

WHAT DID I DO TO DESERVE THIS?

1 Peter 4:12-19

Throughout Peter's letter he has dealt with suffering and persecution. This theme returns to prominence in the last part of the fourth chapter. Peter's emphasis is needed in America today when there is so much emphasis on the so-called "Gospel of Prosperity." I like the title of a recent book, *God Wants You Rich and Other Enticing Myths*. That God desires a trouble-free life for us is a myth, but it is enticing and needs the counteracting of Peter's words.

I'm Suffering: What Went Wrong? (4:12-14)

Peter warns us *not to think it strange* when we suffer (vs 12). The suffering he particularly has in mind is that of persecution for the Christian faith. He describes it as a "fiery" trial, the allusion being to the intense heat of the refiner's furnace (cf 1:7). Such trial is no accident but appointed by God as a way of testing and purifying faith. Christians shouldn't be surprised when they encounter such. Read Paul's description of his trials in 2 Corinthians 11:23-27 or that of the heroes of the faith in Hebrews 11:35-38.

It is easy to see how Christians could think it strange. Does God not love them? Can he not protect them? Has he not promised to be with them?

But the New Testament abounds with warnings to expect persecution, and instructions on the proper response. John wrote, "Do not be surprised, my brothers, if the world hates you" (1 John 3:13, NIV). The antagonism of the world toward true Christianity is so strong it is amazing that the persecution hasn't been worse, and we must be prepared to endure such.

> Must I be carried to the skies
> On flow'ry beds of ease
> While others fought to win the prize,
> And sailed through bloody seas?
>
> — Isaac Watts

Rather than think it strange *we should rejoice,* says Peter (vs 13; cf Matt. 5:10-12). He gives several reasons for such continual rejoicing. First, because we are partakers of Christ's suffering. That doesn't mean that we add anything to Christ's atonement. The sufferings he underwent for our sins were unique and sufficient. Said Jesus, "It is finished!" Rather are we partakers in the sense that our sufferings are the result of our association with Christ. We are his representatives and we prosecute his cause.

The second reason for rejoicing is that, when we suffer with Christ and endure, we can be certain our faith is real and we will be glorified with him. Christ's glory (brightness, splendor) will be revealed (Gk. *apokalupsis,* "unveiled") when he returns; and true Christians, who experienced the antagonism of the world, will be rewarded. For many the event will be terrifying (cf Rev. 6:16) but for the Christian it will be a time of exceeding joy.

> And soon shall come that glorious day
> When, seated on Thy throne,

Thou shalt to wondering worlds display
That we with Thee are one.

—J. G. Deck

As Paul says, "The sufferings of this present time are not worthy to be compared with the glory which shall be revealed in us" (Rom. 8:18).

Not only should we rejoice, but we should *realize that we are blessed* through such suffering (vs 14). The specific nature of some of these trials is now delineated: some Christians will be reproached for the name of Christ. Such reproach is not a misfortune to be resented in self-pity; rather are you "blessed—happy, fortunate, to be envied" (Amp. NT). Again Peter gives his reasons: "For the spirit of glory and of God resteth upon you." It is the fact of the Spirit's influence in your life that has produced the tension between you and the world. Such persecution is the evidence of his working powerfully in and through you (cf Stephen's martyrdom, Acts 6). Moreover the suffering will bring his presence and power to rest in greater measure upon you. In all of this you are glorifying Christ!

I'm Suffering: Did I Do Wrong? (4:15)

Peter warns Christians that these promised blessings are not valid when we bring suffering upon ourselves by our wrongdoing. In his admonition he lists some of the things he has in mind: murder, stealing, evildoing in general and meddling in others' affairs. Whatever penalty we receive for these and similar things is well-deserved. And of course nothing is a greater stumbling block to the nonchristian than seeing those who profess that Christ has changed their lives doing such things.

> You are writing a gospel, a chapter each day,
> By deeds that you do, by words that you say.
> Men read what you write, whether faithless or true.
> Say, what is the gospel according to you?
>
> —Paul Gilbert

The very fact that Peter warns about such crimes has implications for the character of the social environment and the background of these converts. They were expected to live godly lives in a very ungodly society, just as we are.

I'm Suffering: Is My Response Right? (4:16-19)

Peter is concerned that our response to such suffering is correct and constructive. He urges us *not to feel shame* when we suffer for our Christian stance (vs 16). The world has always lashed out at godliness, Christ himself being the supreme example. Rather should we glorify God, praising him for the privilege of suffering for him. The name Christian ("little Christs") is a term of derision in the New Testament and used only three times.

It is important that Christians *maintain a certain perspective* (vss 17, 18). If God judges his own, what will be the end of nonchristians (cf Prov. 11:31)? His judgment of his own falls on them in this life in the form of trials and persecution from a hostile society. He uses such suffering to prove and purify his people. They are scarcely (Gk. *malis,* "copious labor") saved, not in the sense of there being any uncertainty about it—what can separate us from the love of God?—but in reference to the difficulties they endure in the process. These scarcely saved are referred to as "the righteous." We must always keep in mind that there is none righteous as far as our obedience to God's law is concerned, and that the way God reckons men righteous is through faith. Paul elaborates on the process in Romans 3:22-24:

> Even the righteousness of God which is by faith of Jesus Christ unto all and upon all them that believe: for there is no difference: For all have sinned, and come short of the glory of God; Being justified freely by his grace through the redemption that is in Christ Jesus.

If that judgment begins at the house of God, says Peter, what shall be the end of them that obey not the gospel of God? Although we must believe the gospel, Peter doesn't speak of disbelieving but of disobeying. The gospel makes its demand on the will—we either reject the truth or obey it. We can disobey not only by outright rejection but by seeking to combine some righteousness of our own with Christ as our ground of salvation, or by professing faith but living as the world does. The doom that awaits the disobedient is indeed terrible to contemplate.

Having counseled us not to be ashamed and to have the above perspective, Peter urges that we *take certain actions when persecuted*.

First, consider this to be according to the will of God. It is God's way of bringing us into a fuller share of the Spirit's power and presence.

Second, commit the keeping of your soul to him as a faithful Creator. The Greek word for "commit" was used of turning over money to a friend for safekeeping. In Peter's day there were no banks, so a person leaving his home for an extended period would place his valuables in the custody of someone he could trust. We are to place our souls in God's keeping. Jesus used the same term when he said, "Father, into your hands I commit my spirit" (Luke 23:46, NIV). Trust that he will deal with you faithfully even though he's putting you through suffering. He will use this for your good and ultimately glorify you with Christ.

Third, continue to do well — obey God's word. Don't allow yourself to be sidetracked by resentment toward men for their harsh treatment or toward God for his painful providence.

Peter's prescription for the right response couldn't be better summarized than in the old hymn:

> Trust and obey, for there's no other way
> To be happy in Jesus, but to trust and obey.
>
> — James H. Sammis

I'm Suffering: Am I Learning?

How well are we practicing these principles? Are we surprised when we are reproached for our Christian stance as though something strange had happened to us? Do we take such trials with joy, realizing that we are partakers of Christ's suffering and that they are working a far more exceeding and eternal weight of glory? Are we trusting God to cause his Spirit to rest upon us in a fuller way through such trials? Is there any suffering we are bringing upon ourselves by unchristian behavior? Are we trusting and obeying?

Review Questions

1. If we are not to be surprised by persecution, what should our attitude be?
2. In what sense are we partakers of Christ's sufferings?
3. What is the relationship between the promise of future glory and the present suffering of persecution?
4. What connection is there between our suffering persecution and the Holy Spirit's resting upon us?
5. In what sense are the righteous scarcely saved? How can anyone be righteous?

Discussion Questions

1. If a person becomes a Christian and immediately begins to suffer persecution or problems, what kind of thinking could this lead to?
2. What connection do you see between Matthew 5:3-9 and Matthew 5:10-12?
3. What might the absence of persecution indicate?
4. Have you experienced persecution as a Christian? How did your response compare with Peter's instructions here? What good effect can you see that such suffering has had in your life?
5. In enduring suffering for Christ's sake, what has helped you the most?
6. If you were asked to tell a group of new believers what to expect in the Christian life, what are some things you would tell them?

12

MY TURN TO LEAD

1 Peter 5

If there is anything the church needs today it is godly leaders. Peter addresses this subject in his final chapter. When Paul discusses qualifications for leadership in 1 Timothy and Titus he deals mainly with character. Leadership crises are more often caused by character breakdown than by lack of gifts.

Taking responsibility is not easy. I read of a police recruit who was given the following scenario to test his reaction: he has been called to the scene where a crowd is gathered around two men clearly intent on killing each other. Behind them a burglar is breaking into a house. A panic-stricken man grabs him to tell him his wife needs to go to the hospital and the ambulance men are on strike. The recruit can hardly take this in before he notices that a fire is spreading through an apartment building across the street and a woman is screaming for help from a top-floor window. Asked what he would do in such a situation, the recruit wrote: "Take off my uniform and merge with the crowd."

Every church leader is tempted to do that — or, worse, not put on the uniform. But it is crucial that those God has equipped accept the role and responsibilities.

What's a Leader Supposed to Do? (5:1-4)

Peter starts out by covering *the responsibilities of leaders*. He designates the leaders as elders (Greek *presbuteroi*, vs 1). The presbyterian church gets its name from this form of government. The idea of eldership has a long and important history starting when Moses appointed seventy elders to share the responsibilities of leading Israel with him (Num. 11:16-30). From that time on Israel had elders, and in the New Testament church the apostles ordained elders in each church planted (Acts 14:23).

Peter describes himself as a fellow elder and one who had personally witnessed the sufferings of Christ. He also would partake of the glory to be revealed when Christ returns. Peter had a glimpse of this glory when Christ was transfigured.

Peter exhorts the elders in regard to their responsibilities (vss 2-4). First he speaks of what their responsibilities are. They are to feed the flock of God. We naturally think of making sure the flock is nourished adequately on the word of God, and this is part of what is meant. But the word really signifies "act the part of a shepherd" (NIV "be shepherds") — that is, provide food, strengthen the diseased, seek the strays, and so on. Peter doubtless could still hear Christ's words ringing in his ears. "Simon, lovest thou me? Feed my sheep." Peter, by describing the flock as God's, reminds the leaders that they are but undershepherds—it is God's flock, not theirs, and since it is God's every sheep is *very* valuable.

The parallel phrase *taking oversight thereof* reminds us of the governing and protection necessary and also points to shepherding in general.

Second, Peter shows how these responsibilities are to be performed. They are to be done in the right spirit—not because the people involved are forced into it but voluntarily. Grudging leadership produces grudging followers. The flock should see the leaders as models of joyful service. The opposite of a willing spirit is a withholding spirit. God loves a cheerful giver and a willing leader!

These responsibilities are to be done *with the right motive,* not for material gain (self-interest) but out of a desire to serve. This doesn't mean that it is wrong to pay some church leaders (cf 1 Cor. 9:14), but a leadership position should not be sought for personal advantage—because it will enhance my profession, for example. We should aspire to lead from right motives. "To aspire to leadership is an honourable ambition" (1 Tim. 3:1, NEB). The true leader is a "kingdom man," more interested in building God's kingdom than his own particular church or denomination.

It is important that the responsibilities be carried out *in the right manner,* not driving but leading the flock. Leaders are to lead by example. They not only teach tithing, they tithe; they not only speak of witnessing, they witness. As someone has said, "The real problem of Christianity is not atheism or skepticism, but the non-witnessing Christian trying to smuggle his own soul into heaven."

Christ led by example. Taking a towel he washed the disciples' feet and then said, "If I then, your Lord and Master, have washed your feet; ye also ought to wash one another's feet" (John 13:14). It was when he was praying that they said, "Lord, teach us to pray." Jesus repudiated the secular model of leading by lording it over others, saying that greatness came through serving (Matt. 20:25-28).

Third, Peter speaks of *their reward*. This reminds them not only that they must give account to the Chief Shepherd but also that he will reward service done with eternal rewards. *Crown of glory* refers not just to a glorious crown but a share in glory as one's reward.

What's a Follower to Do? (5:5-9)

Having covered the responsibilities of leaders Peter next mentions some responsibilities that all Christians have.

The first is *to be humble* (vss 5, 6). The younger are to submit to the elder, but all are to be subject to one another. They are to "wear the 'overall' of humility in serving each other" (Phillips). Peter gives a strong reason, quoting Proverbs 3:34: "[God] scorneth the scorners: but he giveth grace to the lowly." If men do not humble themselves God sets himself against them. The word is used for a general bringing his army up against an enemy. Think of how God resisted proud Nebuchadnezzar (Dan. 4).

Contrariwise God gives grace to the humble. Thus Peter's counsel: humble yourself under the mighty hand of God. God's hand refers to his providential dealings with us, especially the suffering we may have to endure. Humbling ourselves under his hand means to be aware that he is in control and to yield to and trust him in everything.

Amy Carmichael in poetry expresses different ways we try to handle suffering and heartache, such as by forgetting or busyness or aloofness; but none of these bring peace. Finally,

> He said, "I will accept the breaking sorrow
> Which God tomorrow
> Will to his son explain."
> Then did the turmoil deep within him cease.
> Not vain the word, not vain;
> In acceptance lieth peace.

The prospect is that when we do humble ourselves God will exalt us in due time. Jesus promised, "[H]e that humbleth himself shall be exalted" (Luke 14:11). *In due time* refers to *God's* wisely appointed time, not *our* time.

The second is *to be trustful* (vs 7). You are to cast all your cares upon him (cf Ps. 55:22). You can't get rid of your troubles necessarily but you can "throw the whole weight of your anxieties upon him" (Phillips). The verb tense indicates a single decisive action, but all of us know how difficult it is not to take the burden back upon ourselves. When we find ourselves doing that we must again cast it on the Lord. Jesus encouraged his disciples not to be anxious about food or clothing, for our heavenly Father knows that we need them (Matt. 6:32, NIV). This is similar to Peter's "for he careth for you." Christians begin with the confidence that God does care and he is sovereign; thus anxiety is out of place.

The third responsibility is *to be vigilant* (vss 8, 9). Soberness (self-control) and alertness are urged because of our adversary the devil, who is always looking for an opportunity to devour us. His aim is to get us to stop believing or confessing Christ before the world. The context is that of suffering and we are reminded of the fiery trials many Christians have undergone in persecution for their faith. John says, "[T]hey overcame him by the blood of the Lamb, and by the word of their testimony; and they loved not their lives unto the death" (Rev. 12:11).

Peter's counsel is to resist steadfast in the faith. The reference is probably both to the Christian faith as a body of teaching (that is, by sound doctrine) and to personal trust in God. Again the best defense often is a good offense. Actively sharing our faith as witnessing Christians is a vital part of effective resistance.

Peter adds the further encouragement that you are not alone in your suffering. You have many Christian brothers who are experiencing similar trials and persecution. Be faithful for their sake and take courage from their faithfulness.

What Can I Expect God to Do? (5:10-14)

Peter finishes with a *concluding assurance and personal greetings*. Peter gives assurance that God, who has called them, will strengthen them for the trials (vs 10). His title for God is unique and uplifting: "The God of all grace." I love the poem "He Giveth More":

> He giveth more grace when the burdens grow greater,
> He sendeth more strength when the labors increase;
> To added affliction He addeth His mercies,
> To multiplied trials, His multiplied peace.

His love has no limit, His grace has no measure;
His power no boundary known unto men;
For out of His infinite riches in Jesus
He giveth and giveth and giveth again.

— Annie Johnson Flint

Note what God *has done*: he has called us. These things are said about this calling: it is *by* Christ Jesus; it is *unto* his eternal glory; it is *to find its completion* after we have suffered a little while. The prospect of the future glory should help us to view suffering in perspective. The contrast is between the brief duration of the suffering and the eternal benefit of glory.

Note what God *will do*: he will make us perfect, stablish, strengthen, settle us. The first verb is used of mending nets and means "to make fit or complete." The second indicates "making steadfast," the third "strengthening" or "empowering for active service," and the fourth "settle as on a foundation." All these things God does for the humble, reliant believer. You will have to suffer for a short time, but in time he will bring you into the fulness of his eternal glory.

Reflecting on this, Peter bursts out with praise to God and his eternal power or dominion by which he keeps all things under his control (vs 11).

Peter concludes with personal greetings, mentioning first his secretary or messenger, Silvanus (vs 12). This is apparently the same person Paul refers to as Silas in Acts 15:40. In the face of suffering and trial, he wanted to testify to them that the Christian faith was true and to encourage them to be steadfast in it. He also brings greetings from the church at "Babylon" (probably Rome) and from Mark, and asks God's peace for all true Christians.

How Am I Doing?

Are you aspiring to leadership in God's kingdom or have you been ducking the responsibility through wrong priorities or maybe fear? Perhaps it is your turn to lead. Are you passing it by? If you are a leader, has yours been a willing or reluctant spirit? Is your motive for personal gain or to serve God and others? Have you been leading or driving the sheep? Are you modeling the life-style the sheep need to follow? Are you concerned about nourishing, protecting, shepherding the flock?

For all of us: are we humbling ourselves under God's hand—the circumstances he brings into our lives? Are we trusting him, casting our cares upon him, knowing that he cares for us? Are we vigilant about our old enemy and steadfastly resisting him in Christ's strength?

Review Questions

1. What are the responsibilities of elders? What is implied in the direction to feed the flock and take oversight thereof?
2. From Peter's warnings, what wrong motives and attitudes are often seen in church leadership?
3. Since there is the danger of carrying out the responsibility in the wrong spirit or way, why should any sincere person desire or accept a leadership role?

4. What is meant by "humbling ourselves under the mighty hand of God"?
5. What is Satan's great aim as he attacks Christians?

Discussion Questions

1. What are some ways we can effectively resist Satan?
2. What problems have you encountered with casting all your cares upon God? What has helped in doing this?
3. Can you think of a lay leader who really impacted your life? What characterized his life that made the most impact on you?
4. Of the dangers Peter mentions in regard to wrong approaches to leadership, which do you feel is the most relevant for your particular situation? What can be done to combat the danger?
5. How can we best develop the kind of leaders needed?

13

GETTING IT TOGETHER

We have covered a lot of territory with Peter — everything from bearing mistreatment to bearing witness. The setting, we recall, is the beginning of the Roman persecution of the church; and the chief value of this letter is to show Christians how to live out their Christian commitment under hostile conditions. Let us take a moment and review.

Chapter 1: *More Precious than Gold* (1:1-12)

Peter introduces his theme of suffering, referring to the fiery ordeal his readers were facing. He reminds them of their privileges: elected by God, called by his Spirit, cleansed by Christ's blood. He encourages them with their living hope — founded on Christ's resurrection — of an inheritance in heaven for which they are being kept by God's power. He explains some of God's purposes in putting Christians through such trials: they test and purify our faith. Thus we can rejoice in such trials. How pertinent all this is for us as we face trials today — so often we lose our hope or joy!

On a scale of 1 to 10, rate yourself on your ability to rejoice in suffering and trial. ______

What can you do to move up the scale?

Chapter 2: *Can I Really Be Holy?* (1:13-21)

Peter issues a call to holiness involving a real transformation in conduct. This requires learning to think like a Christian about every area of life: What are the implications of my faith for my job, my home, my social life, my material resources? The essence of holiness is conformity of mind and will with God. Peter's appeal to holiness is based on God's call, his character and his command. He called us out of darkness; he is holy and he commands us to be holy. The life of holiness is a pilgrim life, not seeking my portion in this world; the source of holiness is the Spirit of holiness. Only as we walk in the Spirit can we be holy, but through him we can!

On a scale of 1 to 10, rate yourself on your progress in holiness. ______

What can you do to move up the scale?

Chapter 3: *I Thought I Was Grown Up Already* (1:22-2:3)

Here Peter gives us insight into why so many Christians remain spiritual dwarfs. He exhorts Christians to love that brother Christian! Because Christ has purified our hearts and given us new natures we can do this; but we need to be stirred up to appropriate, loving action. This mark of the Christian is crucial to individual Christian growth as well as to the health of the church. Christians likewise must abstain from sins against such love. Also essential for spiritual growth is the soul food of the word as milk for spiritual babes. This alerts us to the need for a daily quiet time and assimilation of the word through obedience. What is your practice in this area?

On a scale of 1 to 10, rate yourself in the area of loving your brother. ______

In the discipline of a quiet time. ______

What practical steps can you take to improve?

Chapter 4: *How Can a Stone Be Alive?* (2:4-10)

Peter wants us again to appreciate the inestimable privileges that belong to the people of God. Israel had a magnificent temple, but Christians become *part* of a living temple when they come to Christ as living stones. A temple needs a priesthood, and Christians are privileged to perform in this role as they offer spiritual sacrifices through Christ. There is no other approach to God. Those who stumble over Christ's claims and demands of unconditional surrender and holy living will be broken.

By applying to the church terms that were originally used to describe Israel, Peter indicates that Christians are the true Israel of God. The church exists to show forth the praises (virtues) of him who called us out of darkness. To appreciate our privileges we must remember our former condition. Now we are alive in the light, the people of God—before we were the opposite! Is it possible to esteem these privileges too highly?

I'm reminded of the story of the old deacon in the country church who would start shouting during the worship service. The church had a new minister who was trying to create a more dignified atmosphere. Finally a committee visited the deacon one day while he was plowing. He stopped his mules and explained: "Brethren, I know why you're here. I understand we're trying to be more dignified. And every Sunday I resolve not to shout. But then we start to sing 'Amazing Grace,' and I get to thinking how I was lost but now I'm found, I was doomed and now I'm adopted, I'm a child of God, I'm going to heaven, I'm . . . Brethren, *hold these mules while I shout!*"

Do we have any of that spiritual enthusiasm in us?

> On a scale of 1 to 10, rate yourself on your appreciation of the privileges that are yours as a Christian. ________
>
> How could you increase your appreciation?

Chapter 5: *Free to Do What?* (2:11-17)

In contrast to modern ideas of freedom characterized by the throwing off of restraint, Peter says that true freedom is being free to follow a moral life-style. This requires abstaining from fleshly lusts that war against the soul and actively pursuing the good. Christian freedom also involves submitting to proper authority, such as the civil authority. Though free we are always servants of God, and he would have us demonstrate that by abiding by the law. We are to honor all men (*all* are in the image of God) and to love the brotherhood (the church). We are to be active in a local church but support in many ways the church universal.

On a scale of 1 to 10, rate yourself on your attitude toward submitting to authority. ______

On your commitment to the local church. ______

To the church universal. ______

How could you improve your performance in this respect?

Chapter 6: ***It Doesn't Seem Fair*** **(2:18-25)**

In one of the most practical and hard-to-practice sections, Peter discusses how Christians should respond when they are treated unfairly. Many people short-circuit their spiritual fruitfulness right here. The principle again is submission—just *take* it! Such taking it patiently is acceptable with God and is a part of our calling. Peter uses Christ as our example: when he was reviled, he reviled not again.

The reference to Christ's suffering leads to a discussion of the nature of Christ's death as a substitutionary atonement as he bore our sin so that we, being dead to sin, should live unto righteousness. Christ died to make us godly men and women. Each case of mistreatment is an opportunity to practice dying to sin!

On a scale of 1 to 10, rate yourself on your practice of taking it patiently when treated unfairly. ______

What could you do to improve in this area?

Chapter 7: *Isn't My Home My Castle?* (3:1-7)

Peter tackles the crucial area of husband-wife relations. Instead of speaking of the rights of each he speaks of the duties. For the wife the key once more is submission. With an unbelieving husband, the wife should seek to win him to Christ by her behavior "without the word." Her true beauty is found in a meek and quiet spirit instead of being domineering or complaining.

The Christian husband is to be considerate of his wife, remembering her more-sensitive nature and honoring her as a treasure. Peter warns that disharmony in the home can be a grave hindrance to our walk with God.

If you are a wife, rate yourself on a scale of 1 to 10 as to your submission. ______

If a husband, rate your considerateness. ______

What practical steps can you take to increase your rating?

Chapter 8: *Why Not Get Even?* (3:8-12)

Now Peter draws attention to sins that have often troubled the body of Christ. He speaks first of harmony in the church, about which Jesus also prayed in his high priestly prayer. Not that we are expected to compromise in the interest of peace those clearly taught truths on which a genuinely biblical faith is founded; but too often the church has been divided by matters which are not so clearly revealed in Scripture. He goes on to commend a sympathetic spirit, love among the brethren, compassion even toward those outside the church, and humility—virtues that ought to mark those who follow Christ.

How natural it is to want to get back at someone who has hurt us! But we are reminded that if we truly love God we must also truly love our brothers and sisters in the Lord. Getting even is not for the people of God; on the contrary, we ought to be sharing, as far as possible, others' joys and sorrows, their cares and concerns. In this way we will be showing clearly that we are indeed children of our heavenly Father.

How are you at controlling your tongue?

On a scale of 1 to 10, rate yourself on your record for promoting harmony among the members of your church family. _______

For showing love toward those who have hurt you. _______

For curbing your tongue even when provoked. _______

How can you better your record in these important areas?

Chapter 9: *"I Never Know What to Say"* (3:13-22)

Here Peter continues to cover the proper response to persecution. He tells us not to be afraid but to sanctify Christ as Lord in our hearts—that is, cultivate the proper fear of God, reverence him and realize that he is in control. We should be ready to give a reasoned defense for our beliefs, marshaling Christian evidences. Many helpful tools are available and with a little effort we can learn to do this.

> On a scale of 1 to 10, rate yourself on your ability to give a reasoned defense of your beliefs. _______
>
> What steps would lead to improvement?

Chapter 10: *Why Is Everyone Looking at Me That Way?* (4:1-11)

When you become a Christian your life begins to change—and it must, so that you no longer live for sinful human desires but for the will of God. Such change is disturbing to old associates, leading to misunderstanding and persecution. Often, says Peter, they will speak evil of you when you "run not with them to the same excess of riot." Has your life changed in such a way that your associates have felt it?

> On a scale of 1 to 10, rate yourself on the degree of change your associates have sensed in your life and how you have made them aware of your Christian commitment. _______
>
> How do you think you could raise your score in this area?

Chapter 11: *What Did I Do to Deserve This?* (4:12-19)

The theme of persecution and suffering returns to prominence, and Peter warns us not to think it strange when we suffer. Rather should we rejoice in that we are suffering for Christ's sake and that we now have evidence of the genuineness of our faith — and thus assurance of our future glorification. We are blessed as such reproach brings God's presence and power to rest upon us. Peter is concerned that we respond correctly under persecution, considering it to be in accord with the will of God and committing the keeping of our souls to him. But we must be careful not to bring persecution upon ourselves by our wrongdoing.

On a scale of 1 to 10, rate yourself on how you respond to persecution. ______

What would help you respond more biblically?

Chapter 12: *My Turn to Lead* (5:1-14)

In this final chapter Peter covers the responsibilities of church leaders. They are to feed (shepherd) the flock of God, governing and protecting them. This must be done in the right spirit, voluntarily and not for personal interest. They are not to lord it over the flock but lead by example.

Peter also speaks of the responsibilities of all Christians to evidence humility toward each other and to humble themselves under God's providential dealings with them. They should cast their cares upon God, knowing that he cares for them. Moreover they must be vigilant in regard to their old enemy, the devil.

In conclusion Peter seeks to bring us to the proper perspective on suffering, contrasting the brief duration of the suffering with the eternal benefit of glory.

> If you are a church leader, rate yourself on a scale of 1 to 10 as to how you meet Peter's criteria. ______
>
> For others, rate how well you are able to keep suffering in a proper perspective. ______
>
> In what way can you better your performance here?

Review Questions

1. What are some of the major themes of 1 Peter?
2. What is the primary theme?
3. Of what value is suffering to the Christian?
4. On what basis does Peter appeal for holy living and the fulfilling of our varied responsibilities?
5. What are some of our privileges as Christians that Peter mentions?

Discussion Questions

1. In your self-rating, in what two areas did you rate highest? lowest?
2. What one theme seemed the most relevant to your life? why?

3. Peter bases his appeal for holy living on Christ's death for us, God's character, what God has done for us, and our accountability on Judgment Day. Which is the most motivating to you? why?

4. Did you discover some new truth in our study of 1 Peter? Was there some old truth that came home with fresh force?

5. Which of the reasons for suffering mentioned by Peter helps you the most to be patient under such suffering?